Table of Contents

Introduction..

Chapter 1: Christmas Cookies & Edible Gifts.................................12
Gingerbread Men Cookies,,,,,...13
Classic Sugar Cookies with Royal Icing.......................................14
Spiced Shortbread..15
Linzer Cookies...16
Speculoos (Spiced Belgian Cookies)...17
Pfeffernüsse (German Spiced Cookies)...18
Biscotti with Almonds and Cranberries..19
Edible Ornaments...20
DIY Hot Chocolate Kits...21
Layered Cookie Mix: Chocolate Chip Cookies...................................22
Spiced Nut Mixes...23
Homemade Truffles..24
Chocolate-Dipped Treats..25
Chocolate-Dipped Marshmallows..26
Chocolate-Covered Dried Fruits...27
Holiday Flavored Popcorn...28
DIY Cookie Mix Jars..29
Stained Glass Cookies..30
Peppermint Bark..31
Almond Snowball Cookies..32
Holiday Thumbprint Cookies...33

Chapter 2: Festive Cakes, Pies & Tarts ... 34

- Rich Fruitcake ... 35
- German Stollen ... 36
- Italian Panettone ... 37
- Yule Log (Bûche de Noël) ... 38
- Pumpkin Spice Cake ... 39
- Gingerbread Cake with Cream Cheese Frosting ... 40
- Eggnog Cupcakes ... 41
- Peppermint Mocha Cupcakes ... 42
- Mulled Wine Cupcakes ... 43
- Classic Pumpkin Pie ... 44
- Mince Pies ... 45
- Pecan Pie ... 46
- Pear and Almond Tart ... 47
- Cranberry Orange Tart ... 48
- Pavlova with Winter Fruits ... 49
- Christmas Cheesecake ... 50

Chapter 3: Savory Bakes for the Holiday Table ... 51

- **Cheesy Savory Pies** ... 52
- Spinach and Feta Pie ... 52
- Mushroom and Goat Cheese Tart ... 53
- **Festive Quiches:** ... 54
- Bacon and Leek Quiche ... 54
- Roasted Vegetable and Gruyere Quiche ... 55
- **Savory Bread Rolls and Buns:** ... 56
- Parmesan Herb Knots ... 56

Cranberry and Walnut Bread...57

Christmas Appetizer Bakes..58

Puff Pastry Bites 58

Savory Scones...59

Cheese Straws...60

Savory Edible Gift..61

Homemade Crackers..61

Savory Biscotti..62

Spiced Nuts 63

Chapter 4: Specialty Diets – Gluten-Free, Vegan & Dairy-Free Bakes.........64

Gluten-Free Cookies:...65

Almond Flour Snowballs...65

Gluten-Free Ginger Snaps...66

Vegan Christmas Cakes: 67

Egg-Free Fruitcake..67

Vegan Chocolate Yule Log..68

Dairy-Free Desserts 69

Dairy-Free Cheesecake...69

Vegan Pumpkin Pie..70

Allergen-Friendly Gifts...71

Nut-Free Biscotti...71

Vegan Chocolate Bark..72

Substitution Guide: How to Adapt Traditional Recipes for Specialty Diets...73

Chapter 5: Festive Drinks and 75

Classic Mulled Wine..76

Holiday Punch (Non-Alcoholic)..77

Cranberry Rum Punch..78

Spiked Holiday Sangria Punch...79

Champagne Holiday Punch..80

Peppermint Hot Cocoa...81

Spiced Mexican Hot Chocolate...82

Traditional Eggnog Recipe 83

Mulled Apple Cider..84

Chapter 6: Creative Presentation Ideas for Edible Gifts.....................85

Festive Packaging Tips..86

Personalized Gift Tags and Labels..87

Gift Basket Ideas...88

Chapter 7: Leftovers Reimagined..89

Christmas Pudding Truffles: Transform Leftover Christmas Pudding into a New Treat..90

Turkey and Cranberry Hand Pies: Savory Bakes with Holiday Leftovers 91

Fruitcake Bread Pudding: A Cozy Dessert to Use Up Leftovers...........92

Leftover Cookies Crumble: Reusing Cookies for Cheesecake Crusts and More 93

Conclusion...94

The Magic of Festive Baking: Bringing Joy Through Sweets and Savory Treats

The magic of festive baking goes beyond the simple act of mixing ingredients together. It's about creating an atmosphere of warmth and celebration, where every stir of the spoon and every sprinkle of sugar carries the spirit of the season. Baking during the holidays transforms your kitchen into a space filled with joy, excitement, and love.

From the comforting smell of cinnamon and nutmeg to the sight of dough rising in the oven, holiday baking brings a sense of anticipation. It's a sensory experience that evokes memories of past celebrations and creates new traditions for the future. Whether you're baking cookies with your children, preparing an elaborate Christmas cake, or making edible gifts for loved ones, every recipe carries the magic of the season with it.

Festive baking is also about sharing. Whether you're passing a plate of freshly baked cookies around the table or wrapping up a homemade cake as a gift, the act of giving adds an extra layer of meaning to each recipe. It's the smiles, the laughter, and the shared moments that turn these baked goods into something truly special. Baking, in this sense, becomes a way to show love and appreciation, transforming simple ingredients into cherished memories.

Let the magic of festive baking inspire you this holiday season. With each recipe, you're not just making delicious treats—you're creating moments of joy, connection, and celebration.

Holiday Traditions Around the World: How Different Cultures Celebrate with Food

The holiday season is a time when cultures around the world come together to celebrate through food, and each country has its own unique traditions and dishes that reflect its history and values. From rich desserts to savory feasts, the culinary diversity during the holidays is a reflection of the different ways people commemorate this special time of year.

In Germany, the Christmas season is synonymous with Lebkuchen (gingerbread) and Stollen, a fruit-filled bread dusted with powdered sugar. Christmas markets, or Weihnachtsmärkte, feature these traditional treats alongside mulled wine, known as Glühwein, which warms up the cold winter nights.

In Italy, the holiday dinner is often centered around Panettone, a sweet bread studded with dried fruits. Another Italian tradition is the Feast of the Seven Fishes, which is celebrated on Christmas Eve. Families serve a variety of fish dishes, often fried or baked, symbolizing the wait for the birth of Christ.

In Mexico, Tamales are a staple for Christmas celebrations, often accompanied by Atole, a warm, thick drink made from masa (corn dough) and flavored with cinnamon. Mexicans also celebrate with Buñuelos, crispy fried dough coated with sugar and cinnamon, and Ponche Navideño, a spiced fruit punch.

In Sweden, the Christmas table, or Julbord, features dishes like Gravlax (cured salmon), Jansson's Temptation (a creamy potato and anchovy dish), and an array of pickled herring. Desserts include Lussekatter, saffron buns shaped into swirls, traditionally served on St. Lucia's Day.

In the United States and Canada, Christmas traditions vary, but a typical holiday meal often includes roasted turkey or ham, cranberry sauce, and pies, such as pumpkin or pecan. Christmas cookies are a significant part of the celebration, and recipes like sugar cookies and gingerbread are often made as a family activity.

In the United Kingdom, Christmas pudding takes center stage—a rich dessert made with dried fruits and spices, often set aflame with brandy before serving. Mince pies, filled with a mixture of fruits and spices, are another classic treat, as are Yule logs—chocolate sponge cakes rolled and decorated to look like a log.

Each of these traditions showcases how food plays an essential role in celebrating the holidays, not just as sustenance, but as a way to bring people together and preserve cultural heritage. Whether through sweet treats, savory dishes, or symbolic feasts, holiday food around the world tells the story of community, family, and the joy of sharing.

Essential Baking Tools and Ingredients for the Holiday Season

The holiday season is the perfect time to whip up festive treats, and having the right tools and ingredients on hand can make all the difference in ensuring your baking is both efficient and enjoyable. Whether you're a seasoned baker or a beginner, here are the essentials you'll need to create everything from Christmas cookies to showstopping cakes.

Baking Tools

Mixing Bowls

A good set of mixing bowls is essential for combining ingredients. Opt for multiple sizes to handle both small and large batches of dough, batter, or icing.

Stand Mixer or Hand Mixer

For holiday baking, where you'll likely be making large quantities of cookies, cakes, and breads, a stand mixer with multiple attachments (paddle, whisk, dough hook) can save time and effort. A hand mixer is a more compact, affordable option.

Measuring Cups and Spoons

Precision is key in baking. Use a set of measuring cups (for dry and liquid ingredients) and spoons to ensure accurate measurements.

Silicone Spatula

A heat-resistant silicone spatula is a must for scraping batter from bowls or folding delicate ingredients like whipped cream or egg whites into mixtures.

Rolling Pin
Essential for rolling out cookie dough, pie crusts, or pastry. A wooden or marble rolling pin works best for even, smooth dough

Baking Sheets and Parchment Paper
Quality baking sheets are crucial for cookies, pastries, and other baked goods. Line them with parchment paper or silicone baking mats for easy cleanup and to prevent sticking.

Cooling Racks
Cooling racks allow baked goods to cool evenly and prevent sogginess. Invest in a couple of wire racks to save countertop space during busy holiday baking sessions.

Cookie Cutters
Festive cookie cutters in shapes like stars, snowflakes, Christmas trees, and gingerbread men are essential for creating holiday-themed cookies.

Pastry Bags and Tips
For piping frosting, decorating cookies, or filling pastries, a pastry bag set with various tips is useful for adding intricate designs to your treats.

Springform Pans and Pie Dishes
For holiday cakes and cheesecakes, a springform pan is ideal for easy release. Pie dishes, preferably glass or ceramic, ensure even baking for holiday pies.

Essential Ingredients
Flour
A versatile, all-purpose flour is the base for most holiday baked goods. For specialized recipes, stock up on whole wheat, gluten-free, or cake flour.

Sugar

Granulated sugar is the go-to for most recipes, but powdered sugar is essential for frostings and glazes, while brown sugar adds moisture and depth of flavor to cookies and cakes.

Spices

Festive spices like cinnamon, nutmeg, ginger, and cloves are key ingredients for creating that warm, holiday flavor in cookies, cakes, and pies.

Butter

Unsalted butter is preferred for baking since it allows for better control over the salt content in your recipes. Make sure it's room temperature for creaming, but cold for pastry doughs.

Eggs

Eggs are essential for structure and texture in most baked goods. Make sure to use large eggs and allow them to come to room temperature for even incorporation into batters and doughs.

Leaveners (Baking Soda, Baking Powder, Yeast)

Baking soda and baking powder are necessary for cookies, cakes, and breads to rise properly. Yeast is essential for making holiday breads and rolls.

Vanilla Extract

Pure vanilla extract enhances the flavor of nearly every baked good. You can also experiment with almond extract or other flavorings for a unique twist.

Chocolate

Stock up on good-quality chocolate (semi-sweet, dark, milk, or white) for cookies, cakes, and confections. Chocolate chips, baking bars, and cocoa powder are all useful for holiday baking.

Dried Fruits and Nuts

Popular for holiday baking, dried fruits like cranberries, raisins, and dates add sweetness and texture to cookies, cakes, and breads. Nuts like almonds, pecans, and walnuts provide crunch and flavor.

Molasses and Honey

Molasses is essential for gingerbread cookies and other spiced baked goods, while honey can be used as a natural sweetener in cakes and breads.

Chapter 1: Christmas Cookies & Edible Gifts

The holidays are a time of giving, and few things are more heartfelt than homemade treats. Whether you're baking classic cookies or preparing unique edible gifts, these creations offer a personal touch that store-bought gifts simply can't match. In this chapter, you'll find a variety of recipes that are perfect for sharing, gifting, or simply enjoying with loved ones. So, gather your ingredients and let the holiday baking begin!

This chapter will provide everything readers need to create beautiful and delicious gifts for their loved ones. Each recipe is simple yet impactful, and the variety ensures there's something for everyone's taste. From classic cookies to creative edible ornaments, these recipes are designed to bring joy and festive cheer to any kitchen.

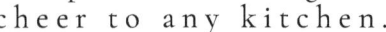

Gingerbread Men Cookies

24 cookies | 15 minutes

Calories per Serving: 150 kcal
Proteins: 2g
Fats: 5g
Carbs: 23g

INGREDIENTS

3 cups all-purpose flour (360g)
3/4 cup brown sugar, packed (150g)
1/2 cup unsalted butter, softened (115g)
1/2 cup molasses (120ml)
1 large egg
1 teaspoon vanilla extract (5ml)
1 tablespoon ground ginger (15g)
1 teaspoon ground cinnamon (5g)
1/4 teaspoon ground cloves (1g)
1/4 teaspoon ground nutmeg (1g)
1 teaspoon baking soda (5g)
1/2 teaspoon salt
Icing and decorations (optional)

NOTES

For a more spiced flavor, increase the amount of ginger and cinnamon.
Store the cookies in an airtight container for up to 5 days.
You can freeze the cookie dough for up to 3 months—just thaw in the fridge overnight before rolling and baking.

DIRECTIONS

1. Preheat the oven to 350°F (180°C). Line two baking sheets with parchment paper.
2. In a large bowl, whisk together the flour, ginger, cinnamon, cloves, nutmeg, baking soda, and salt.
3. In another bowl, cream the butter and brown sugar together until light and fluffy. Beat in the molasses, egg, and vanilla extract until well combined.
4. Gradually add the dry ingredients to the wet ingredients, mixing until a smooth dough forms.
5. Divide the dough in half, flatten into disks, and wrap in plastic wrap. Chill in the refrigerator for at least 1 hour.
6. Roll out the dough on a lightly floured surface to about 1/4 inch thickness. Use gingerbread men cookie cutters to cut out shapes, placing them about 2 inches apart on the prepared baking sheets.
7. Bake for 10-12 minutes, or until the edges are set but the centers are still soft. Let the cookies cool on the baking sheets for 5 minutes before transferring them to wire racks to cool completely.
8. Decorate with icing and other festive decorations as desired.

Classic Sugar Cookies with Royal Icing

 24 cookies   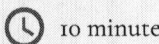 10 minutes

Calories per Serving: 120 kcal
Proteins: 2g
Fats: 5g
Carbs: 18g

INGREDIENTS

For the Sugar Cookies:
2 3/4 cups all-purpose flour (330g)
1 cup unsalted butter, softened (230g)
1 cup granulated sugar (200g)
1 large egg
2 teaspoons vanilla extract (10ml)
1/2 teaspoon almond extract (optional)
1 teaspoon baking powder (5g)
1/4 teaspoon salt

For the Royal Icing:
3 cups powdered sugar (360g)
2 tablespoons meringue powder (30g) or 2 large egg whites
5-6 tablespoons water (adjust to desired consistency)
Gel food coloring (optional)

NOTES
For a crisper cookie, roll the dough slightly thinner. For a softer cookie, roll it thicker. Royal icing will keep in an airtight container in the fridge for up to 3 days. Store decorated cookies in an airtight container at room temperature for up to a week.

DIRECTIONS

1. Preheat the oven to 350°F (180°C). Line baking sheets with parchment paper.
2. In a medium bowl, whisk together the flour, baking powder, and salt.
3. In a large bowl, cream the butter and sugar together until light and fluffy. Beat in the egg, vanilla extract, and almond extract (if using).
4. Gradually add the dry ingredients to the wet ingredients, mixing until a soft dough forms.
5. Roll out the dough on a lightly floured surface to about 1/4-inch thickness. Use cookie cutters to cut into desired shapes and place them on the prepared baking sheets.
6. Bake for 8-10 minutes or until the edges are lightly golden. Let the cookies cool on the baking sheets for 5 minutes before transferring them to a wire rack to cool completely.

For the Royal Icing:
1. In a bowl, whisk together the powdered sugar, meringue powder (or egg whites), and water. Adjust the consistency by adding more water for a thinner glaze or more powdered sugar for a thicker icing.
2. Divide the icing into separate bowls and add food coloring, if desired.
3. Use a piping bag or squeeze bottle to decorate the cooled cookies with the royal icing. Let the icing set for at least 1 hour before serving or packaging.

Spiced Shortbread

24 cookies　　15 minutes

Calories per Serving: 140 kcal
Proteins: 2g
Fats: 7g
Carbs: 18g

INGREDIENTS

2 cups all-purpose flour (240g)
1/2 cup granulated sugar (100g)
1 cup unsalted butter, softened (230g)
1 teaspoon ground cinnamon (5g)
1/2 teaspoon ground nutmeg (2g)
1/4 teaspoon ground cloves (1g)
1/2 teaspoon vanilla extract (2.5ml)
1/4 teaspoon salt
Extra sugar for sprinkling (optional)

DIRECTIONS

1. Preheat the oven to 325°F (160°C). Line two baking sheets with parchment paper.
2. In a large bowl, cream together the butter and sugar until light and fluffy.
3. Stir in the vanilla extract, cinnamon, nutmeg, cloves, and salt until well combined.
4. Gradually add the flour, mixing until a soft dough forms.
5. Roll the dough out on a lightly floured surface to about 1/4-inch thickness. Use a cookie cutter to create shapes such as stars, hearts, or classic rounds.
6. Place the shortbread on the prepared baking sheets, spacing them about 1 inch apart.
7. Sprinkle the tops with a little extra sugar, if desired, and bake for 12-15 minutes, or until the edges are lightly golden.
8. Let the cookies cool on the baking sheets for 5 minutes, then transfer to a wire rack to cool completely.

NOTES

These cookies make excellent edible gifts when packaged in festive tins or wrapped in cellophane bags with decorative ribbons.
For a personalized touch, add a small gift tag with a handwritten message.
Shortbread cookies stay fresh for up to a week when stored in an airtight container, making them perfect for gifting in advance.

Linzer Cookies

 24 cookies   12 minutes

Calories per Serving: 170 kcal
Proteins: 2g
Fats: 9g
Carbs: 21g

INGREDIENTS

1 1/2 cups all-purpose flour (180g)
1/2 cup ground almonds (60g)
1/2 cup unsalted butter, softened (115g)
1/2 cup granulated sugar (100g)
1 large egg yolk
1 teaspoon vanilla extract (5ml)
1/2 teaspoon ground cinnamon (2g)
Pinch of salt
1/2 cup raspberry or strawberry jam (120g)
Powdered sugar for dusting

NOTES

Linzer cookies make beautiful edible gifts when stacked in decorative boxes or wrapped in parchment and tied with ribbon. They can be prepared a few days in advance, as the flavor improves with time.
For variety, try using different jams like apricot or blackberry to suit your preferences.
This Linzer cookie recipe highlights its potential as a charming holiday gift, offering packaging tips and ideas for customization.

DIRECTIONS

1. Preheat the oven to 350°F (180°C). Line two baking sheets with parchment paper.
2. In a medium bowl, whisk together the flour, ground almonds, cinnamon, and salt.
3. In a large bowl, cream the butter and sugar together until light and fluffy. Add the egg yolk and vanilla extract, mixing until well combined.
4. Gradually add the dry ingredients to the wet mixture, stirring until a soft dough forms.
5. Divide the dough into two portions, flatten each into a disk, and wrap in plastic wrap. Chill the dough for at least 1 hour.
6. Roll out one disk of dough on a lightly floured surface to about 1/8-inch thickness. Use a round cookie cutter to cut out the base cookies, placing them on the prepared baking sheets.
7. Roll out the second disk and cut out the tops, using a smaller cutter to create a window in the center (such as a star or heart).
8. Bake both the base and top cookies for 10-12 minutes, or until the edges are lightly golden. Let the cookies cool on the baking sheets for 5 minutes before transferring to a wire rack to cool completely.
9. Spread about 1 teaspoon of jam on each base cookie, then gently press a window cookie on top to create a sandwich.
10. Dust the finished cookies with powdered sugar before serving or packaging.

Speculoos (Spiced Belgian Cookies)

 30 cookies   🕒 12 minutes

Calories per Serving: 100 kcal
Proteins: 1g
Fats: 4g
Carbs: 14g

INGREDIENTS

2 cups all-purpose flour (240g)
3/4 cup brown sugar, packed (150g)
1/2 cup unsalted butter, softened (115g)
1 large egg
2 teaspoons ground cinnamon (10g)
1/4 teaspoon ground nutmeg (1g)
1/4 teaspoon ground cloves (1g)
1/2 teaspoon ground ginger (2g)
1/2 teaspoon ground cardamom (2g)
1/4 teaspoon salt
1 teaspoon baking soda (5g)
2 tablespoons milk (30ml)

DIRECTIONS

1. Preheat the oven to 350°F (180°C). Line two baking sheets with parchment paper.
2. In a medium bowl, whisk together the flour, baking soda, salt, cinnamon, nutmeg, cloves, ginger, and cardamom.
3. In a separate bowl, cream the butter and brown sugar together until smooth. Add the egg and milk, and mix until combined.
4. Gradually add the dry ingredients to the wet ingredients, mixing until a soft dough forms.
5. Roll out the dough on a lightly floured surface to about 1/4-inch thickness. Use festive cookie cutters to cut out shapes like stars or trees, and place them on the prepared baking sheets.
6. Bake for 10-12 minutes, or until the edges are golden brown. Let the cookies cool on the baking sheets for 5 minutes, then transfer to a wire rack to cool completely.
7. Once cooled, store the cookies in an airtight container or package them as edible gifts in festive tins or cellophane bags.

NOTES

Speculoos cookies are known for their rich spice blend, making them perfect for gifting during the holidays.
These cookies keep well and are ideal for shipping or storing for several weeks.
For an extra touch, dust the cookies lightly with powdered sugar or drizzle with melted chocolate.

Pfeffernüsse (German Spiced Cookies)

 30 cookies   12 minutes

Calories per Serving: 110 kcal
Proteins: 2g
Fats: 3g
Carbs: 18g

INGREDIENTS

2 cups all-purpose flour (240g)
1/2 cup brown sugar, packed (100g)
1/4 cup honey or molasses (60ml)
1 large egg
1 teaspoon ground cinnamon (5g)
1/2 teaspoon ground nutmeg (2g)
1/2 teaspoon ground cloves (2g)
1/2 teaspoon ground ginger (2g)
1/4 teaspoon ground black pepper (1g)
1/2 teaspoon baking powder (2g)
1/2 teaspoon baking soda (2g)
1/4 teaspoon salt
Powdered sugar for rolling (about 1/2 cup)

DIRECTIONS

1. Preheat the oven to 350°F (180°C). Line a baking sheet with parchment paper.
2. In a medium bowl, whisk together the flour, baking powder, baking soda, salt, cinnamon, nutmeg, cloves, ginger, and black pepper.
3. In a separate bowl, beat together the brown sugar, egg, and honey (or molasses) until smooth and creamy.
4. Gradually add the dry ingredients to the wet ingredients, mixing until a thick dough forms.
5. Roll the dough into small, walnut-sized balls and place them about 2 inches apart on the prepared baking sheet.
6. Bake for 12-15 minutes, or until the cookies are lightly golden and firm to the touch.
7. Remove from the oven and let the cookies cool slightly, then roll them in powdered sugar while they are still warm.
8. Allow the cookies to cool completely before serving or packaging.

NOTES

Pfeffernüsse cookies are traditionally spiced and are known for their soft, chewy texture. They make perfect gifts when packaged in decorative tins or holiday-themed boxes.
The flavor of these cookies improves over time, so consider baking them a few days before gifting

Biscotti with Almonds and Cranberries

🍴 24 biscotti 🕐 40 minutes

Calories per Serving: 150 kcal
Proteins: 3g
Fats: 6g
Carbs: 21g

INGREDIENTS
2 cups all-purpose flour (240g)
1 cup granulated sugar (200g)
1 teaspoon baking powder (5g)
1/4 teaspoon salt
3 large eggs
1 teaspoon vanilla extract (5ml)
1/2 teaspoon almond extract (optional)
1 cup dried cranberries (120g)
3/4 cup whole almonds, toasted and roughly chopped (90g)

NOTES
For a more festive touch, you can drizzle the biscotti with melted white chocolate once they have cooled.
Store biscotti in an airtight container for up to two weeks, making them ideal for preparing in advance for holiday gifting.

DIRECTIONS
1. Preheat the oven to 350°F (180°C). Line a baking sheet with parchment paper.
2. In a medium bowl, whisk together the flour, sugar, baking powder, and salt.
3. In a separate large bowl, beat the eggs, vanilla extract, and almond extract (if using) until combined.
4. Gradually add the dry ingredients to the wet ingredients, mixing until a sticky dough forms.
5. Stir in the dried cranberries and chopped almonds until evenly distributed throughout the dough.
6. On a floured surface, divide the dough in half and shape each half into a log about 12 inches long and 2 inches wide. Place the logs on the prepared baking sheet, leaving space between them.
7. Bake for 30-35 minutes, or until the logs are firm to the touch and lightly golden. Remove from the oven and let cool for 10 minutes.
8. Using a serrated knife, slice the logs diagonally into 1/2-inch thick biscotti pieces. Lay the slices cut-side down on the baking sheet.
9. Return the biscotti to the oven and bake for an additional 10-12 minutes, flipping halfway through, until both sides are crisp and golden.
10. Allow the biscotti to cool completely before serving or packaging as edible gifts.

Edible Ornaments

 24 cookies   12 minutes

Calories per
Serving: 130 kcal
Proteins: 2g
Fats: 4g
Carbs: 22g

INGREDIENTS

2 1/2 cups all-purpose flour (300g)
1/2 cup granulated sugar (100g)
1 cup unsalted butter, softened (230g)
1 large egg
1 teaspoon vanilla extract (5ml)
1/4 teaspoon salt
1/4 teaspoon ground cinnamon (optional)
1/2 teaspoon baking powder (2.5g)
Hard candies (such as Jolly Ranchers or lifesavers), crushed
Icing and decorations (optional)

NOTES

For best results, make sure the hole for hanging is large enough, as it may shrink slightly during baking.
Store the cookies in an airtight container for up to a week, or wrap them individually and freeze them for longer storage.

DIRECTIONS

1. Preheat the oven to 350°F (180°C). Line two baking sheets with parchment paper.
2. In a large bowl, cream together the butter and sugar until light and fluffy. Beat in the egg and vanilla extract.
3. In another bowl, whisk together the flour, salt, baking powder, and cinnamon (if using).
4. Gradually add the dry ingredients to the wet mixture, stirring until a dough forms.
5. Roll the dough out on a lightly floured surface to about 1/4-inch thickness. Use festive cookie cutters (stars, hearts, snowflakes) to cut out shapes.
6. Transfer the cookies to the prepared baking sheets, and use a smaller cutter or a straw to cut a small hole at the top of each cookie for hanging.
7. Fill the center of each cookie with crushed hard candies.
8. Bake for 10-12 minutes, or until the edges are lightly golden and the candy centers have melted into a stained-glass effect.
9. Allow the cookies to cool completely on the baking sheet before handling. Once cooled, decorate with icing and other embellishments if desired.
10. Thread ribbons through the holes, turning these cookies into edible ornaments ready for gifting or hanging on your Christmas tree.

DIY Hot Chocolate Kits

🍴 4 kits   🕐 10 minutes

Calories per Serving: 180 kcal
Proteins: 2g
Fats: 3g
Carbs: 22g

INGREDIENTS
1/2 cup cocoa powder (unsweetened) (50g)

1/2 cup powdered sugar (60g)

1/4 cup chocolate chips (milk, dark, or white) (50g)

1/4 teaspoon ground cinnamon (optional)

1/4 teaspoon salt

Mini marshmallows (about 1/4 cup per kit)

Crushed candy canes (optional)

Extras: chocolate sprinkles, whipped cream powder, or any favorite topping

NOTES
For a dairy-free version, suggest using almond, coconut, or oat milk with the hot chocolate mix.

These kits can be assembled in advance and stored for up to a month in a cool, dry place, making them perfect for gifting throughout the holiday season.

DIRECTIONS

Instructions for Assembly:

1. Layering the Kit: In a clear mason jar or decorative bag, layer the cocoa powder first, followed by powdered sugar, and then chocolate chips. If using cinnamon or other flavorings, add them on top of the chocolate chips.
2. Marshmallow Topper: Add mini marshmallows as the final layer. For a festive touch, you can also include crushed candy canes or other toppings like chocolate sprinkles or whipped cream powder.
3. Seal the Jar: Close the jar tightly with a lid, or if using a bag, tie it securely with a festive ribbon.

Instructions for Use (to be included in the gift):

1. Heat 2 cups (480ml) of milk (or water) in a saucepan until warm.
2. Stir in the contents of the jar or bag and simmer for 2-3 minutes, stirring constantly until the mixture is smooth and creamy.
3. Pour into mugs and top with extra marshmallows or whipped cream if desired.

Layered Cookie Mix: Chocolate Chip Cookies

🍴 24 cookies 🕐 10 minutes

Calories per Serving: 120 kcal
Proteins: 2g
Fats: 6g
Carbs: 18g

INGREDIENTS
1 3/4 cups all-purpose flour (210g)
3/4 teaspoon baking soda (3.5g)
3/4 teaspoon baking powder (3.5g)
1/2 teaspoon salt
3/4 cup brown sugar, packed (150g)
3/4 cup granulated sugar (150g)
1 cup chocolate chips (180g)
Optional: 1/2 cup rolled oats (50g), 1/2 cup chopped nuts (60g), or festive sprinkles

DIRECTIONS
1. Preheat the oven to 350°F (180°C). Line a baking sheet with parchment paper.
2. In a large bowl, empty the jar contents and mix together the flour, baking soda, baking powder, and salt.
3. In a separate large bowl, whisk together 1/2 cup melted butter, 1 large egg, and 1 teaspoon vanilla extract until well combined.
4. Gradually add the dry ingredients to the wet ingredients, mixing until a dough forms.
5. Scoop out tablespoon-sized portions of dough onto the prepared baking sheet, leaving 2 inches between cookies.
6. Bake for 10-12 minutes or until the edges are golden brown. Let cool on the sheet for 5 minutes before transferring to a wire rack.

NOTES
This layered cookie mix makes for an excellent holiday gift. Package the ingredients in a mason jar with a festive ribbon and attach a tag with baking instructions.
You can customize the recipe with white chocolate chips, dried cranberries, or sprinkles for a more festive touch.
Store baked cookies in an airtight container for up to one week.

Spiced Nut Mixes

🍴 2 cups 🕐 25 minutes

Calories per Serving: 200 kcal
Proteins: 5g
Fats: 18g
Carbs: 6g

INGREDIENTS
2 cups mixed nuts (almonds, walnuts, pecans, or cashews)

2 tablespoons olive oil or melted butter

1 tablespoon brown sugar

1 teaspoon ground cumin

1/2 teaspoon smoked paprika

1/4 teaspoon cayenne pepper (optional for heat)

1/2 teaspoon salt

1/4 teaspoon black pepper

NOTES
These Spiced Nut Mixes are ideal for holiday gifting. Package them in small glass jars or festive cellophane bags tied with ribbon for a seasonal touch.

For a sweeter variation, increase the brown sugar and add a touch of cinnamon.

Store in an airtight container for up to two weeks, making them perfect for preparing in advance.

DIRECTIONS

1. Preheat the oven to 350°F (175°C). Line a baking sheet with parchment paper.
2. In a large bowl, toss the mixed nuts with olive oil or melted butter, ensuring they are evenly coated.
3. In a separate bowl, mix together the brown sugar, cumin, smoked paprika, cayenne pepper (if using), salt, and black pepper.
4. Add the spice mixture to the nuts, tossing until evenly coated.
5. Spread the spiced nuts on the prepared baking sheet in a single layer.
6. Bake for 20-25 minutes, stirring halfway through to ensure even toasting.
7. Remove from the oven and allow the nuts to cool completely before serving or packaging.

Homemade Truffles

🍴 24 truffles   🕒 25 minutes

Calories per Serving: 100 kcal
Proteins: 1g
Fats: 7g
Carbs: 8g

INGREDIENTS

2 8 oz semi-sweet or dark chocolate (230g), finely chopped
1/2 cup heavy cream (120ml)
1 teaspoon vanilla extract (5ml) or any flavoring of choice (e.g., orange, peppermint)
2 tablespoons unsalted butter, softened (30g)
Cocoa powder, chopped nuts, shredded coconut, or sprinkles for coating

DIRECTIONS

1. Heat the cream: In a small saucepan, heat the heavy cream over medium heat until it just begins to simmer. Remove from heat.
2. Melt the chocolate: Place the chopped chocolate in a heatproof bowl. Pour the hot cream over the chocolate and let sit for 1-2 minutes. Stir gently until the chocolate is completely melted and smooth.
3. Add flavor and butter: Stir in the vanilla extract (or other flavoring) and the softened butter until fully incorporated.
4. Chill the mixture: Cover the bowl and refrigerate for about 1 hour, or until the mixture is firm enough to scoop.
5. Form the truffles: Once chilled, use a small cookie scoop or teaspoon to portion out the chocolate mixture. Roll each portion into a ball between your palms.
6. Coat the truffles: Roll the truffles in your choice of coating—cocoa powder, chopped nuts, shredded coconut, or sprinkles.
7. Serve or package: Store the truffles in an airtight container in the refrigerator until ready to gift.

NOTES

Truffles can be flavored in various ways—try adding peppermint extract, orange zest, or a splash of liqueur (such as Grand Marnier or Baileys) for different flavor profiles.
Store the truffles in an airtight container in the refrigerator for up to 2 weeks or freeze for longer storage.

Chocolate-Dipped Treats

🍴 24 pretzels 🕐 20 minutes

Calories per Serving: 150 kcal
Proteins: 2g
Fats: 7g
Carbs: 20g

INGREDIENTS

2 1 1/2 cups semi-sweet or dark chocolate chips (340g)
1 1/2 cups white chocolate chips (340g)
24 large pretzel rods (or pretzel twists)
1/4 cup sprinkles, crushed nuts, shredded coconut, or crushed candy canes (optional) for decorating

DIRECTIONS

1. Melt the chocolate: In two separate bowls, melt the semi-sweet/dark chocolate and white chocolate in the microwave, using 30-second intervals, stirring after each interval until smooth. Alternatively, use a double boiler.
2. Dip the pretzels: Dip each pretzel rod (or twist) halfway into the melted chocolate, letting the excess chocolate drip off. Place the dipped pretzels on a baking sheet lined with parchment paper.
3. Decorate: Before the chocolate hardens, sprinkle with your choice of toppings—sprinkles, crushed nuts, coconut, or candy canes for a festive touch.
4. Cool the pretzels: Let the chocolate-dipped pretzels cool and harden at room temperature or refrigerate for 10-15 minutes until firm.
5. Package or serve: Once the pretzels are set, they are ready to serve or be packaged as holiday gifts.

NOTES

These pretzels make great last-minute gifts since they can be prepared and decorated quickly.

Experiment with different types of chocolate (milk, dark, or flavored varieties) to suit different tastes.

Pretzels will keep in an airtight container at room temperature for up to a week, making them ideal for gifting.

Chocolate-Dipped Marshmallows

 24 marshm   20 minutes

Calories per Serving: 110 kcal
Proteins: 1g
Fats: 5g
Carbs: 15g

INGREDIENTS

1 1/2 cups semi-sweet or dark chocolate chips (340g)
1 1/2 cups white chocolate chips (340g)
24 large marshmallows
1/4 cup sprinkles, crushed nuts, shredded coconut, or crushed candy canes (optional) for decorating

DIRECTIONS

1. Melt the chocolate: In two separate bowls, melt the semi-sweet/dark chocolate and white chocolate in the microwave, using 30-second intervals, stirring after each interval until smooth. Alternatively, melt the chocolate using a double boiler.
2. Dip the marshmallows: Insert a skewer or lollipop stick into each marshmallow. Dip each marshmallow halfway into the melted chocolate, letting the excess chocolate drip off. Place the dipped marshmallows on a baking sheet lined with parchment paper.
3. Decorate: Before the chocolate hardens, sprinkle with your choice of toppings—sprinkles, crushed nuts, coconut, or candy canes for a festive touch.
4. Cool the marshmallows: Let the chocolate-dipped marshmallows cool and harden at room temperature or refrigerate for 10-15 minutes until firm.
5. Package or serve: Once the marshmallows are set, they are ready to serve or be packaged as holiday gifts.

NOTES

These marshmallows can be made ahead and stored in an airtight container at room temperature for up to a week, making them a great option for gifting. Experiment with different types of marshmallows, such as mini or flavored marshmallows, for added variety.
This Chocolate-Dipped Marshmallows recipe is simple, fun, and versatile for creating holiday gifts with plenty of creative presentation ideas.

Chocolate-Covered Dried Fruits

24 pieces   20 minutes

Calories per Serving: 90 kcal
Proteins: 1g
Fats: 4g
Carbs: 14g

INGREDIENTS

1 1/2 cups semi-sweet or dark chocolate chips (340g)

24 pieces of dried fruits (apricots, figs, or dates)

1/4 cup crushed nuts, shredded coconut, or sea salt for decoration (optional)

NOTES

Dried fruits such as apricots, figs, and dates are perfect for this recipe, but you can also experiment with dried cherries, mangoes, or pears for variety.
Chocolate-covered dried fruits can be stored in an airtight container for up to 2 weeks, making them an excellent make-ahead option for holiday gifting.

DIRECTIONS

1. Melt the chocolate: In a heatproof bowl, melt the semi-sweet or dark chocolate in the microwave, using 30-second intervals, stirring after each interval until smooth. Alternatively, melt the chocolate using a double boiler.
2. Dip the dried fruits: Dip each dried fruit piece halfway into the melted chocolate, letting the excess chocolate drip off. Place the dipped fruits on a baking sheet lined with parchment paper.
3. Decorate: Before the chocolate hardens, sprinkle the dipped fruits with your choice of toppings—crushed nuts, shredded coconut, or sea salt for a contrast in flavor.
4. Cool the fruits: Let the chocolate-covered fruits cool and harden at room temperature or refrigerate for 10-15 minutes until firm.
5. Package or serve: Once the fruits are set, they are ready to serve or be packaged as holiday gifts.

Holiday Flavored Popcorn

8 cups   🕒 20 minutes

Calories per Serving: 120 kcal
Proteins: 2g
Fats: 4g
Carbs: 18g

INGREDIENTS

8 cups popped popcorn (from about 1/3 cup unpopped kernels)
1/2 cup white chocolate chips (120g), melted
1/2 cup semi-sweet chocolate chips (120g), melted (optional)
1/4 cup crushed candy canes or peppermint candies (optional)
1/4 cup sprinkles (optional)
1/2 teaspoon ground cinnamon (optional for a spiced version)
1/4 cup nuts (optional for added crunch)

NOTES
Customize your holiday popcorn with different flavors: try spicing it up with cinnamon and sugar for a snickerdoodle version, or add cocoa powder for a chocolatey twist.
Store the popcorn in an airtight container for up to a week to maintain freshness, making it a convenient make-ahead gift option.
Experiment with different toppings such as dried cranberries, mini marshmallows, or toffee bits for added texture and flavor.

DIRECTIONS

1. Pop the popcorn: Pop your kernels using an air popper or stovetop method and transfer to a large mixing bowl. Ensure no unpopped kernels remain.
2. Melt the chocolate: Melt the white chocolate and semi-sweet chocolate separately in the microwave in 30-second intervals, stirring until smooth.
3. Coat the popcorn: Drizzle the melted white chocolate over the popcorn and toss to coat evenly. For a mixed chocolate version, drizzle the semi-sweet chocolate as well.
4. Add holiday flavors: Sprinkle the popcorn with crushed candy canes, sprinkles, cinnamon, and nuts (if using) for a festive twist.
5. Cool the popcorn: Spread the popcorn onto a lined baking sheet and allow the chocolate to set at room temperature or refrigerate for 10-15 minutes.
6. Package or serve: Once the popcorn is set, it's ready to serve or package as a holiday gift.

DIY Cookie Mix Jars

 24 cookies   10 minutes

Calories per 1 cookie: 140 kcal
Proteins: 2g
Fats: 6g
Carbs: 20g

INGREDIENTS

1 3/4 cups all-purpose flour (210g)
1/2 teaspoon baking soda
1/4 teaspoon salt
3/4 cup brown sugar, packed (150g)
1/2 cup granulated sugar (100g)
1 cup chocolate chips (170g)
1/2 cup chopped nuts (optional) (60g)

DIRECTIONS

1. Layer the dry ingredients: Start by adding the flour, baking soda, and salt to the bottom of a 1-liter mason jar. Follow with the brown sugar, granulated sugar, chocolate chips, and chopped nuts (if using), creating distinct layers.
2. Seal the jar: Once the jar is filled, seal it tightly with the lid. Make sure the layers stay neat and don't mix.
3. Tag Instructions for the Recipient (Attach to the Jar):
4. Preheat the oven to 350°F (180°C).
5. In a large bowl, combine the contents of the jar with 3/4 cup (170g) unsalted butter, melted, 1 large egg, and 1 teaspoon vanilla extract.
6. Mix until a dough forms.
7. Drop spoonfuls of dough onto a parchment-lined baking sheet and bake for 10-12 minutes, or until the edges are lightly golden.
8. Allow to cool on the baking sheet for 5 minutes, then transfer to a wire rack to cool completely.

NOTES

You can swap out the chocolate chips for other mix-ins such as white chocolate, dried cranberries, or toffee bits to customize the flavor.

Store the jar in a cool, dry place, and it will keep for several weeks, making it a perfect make-ahead gift option.

Include options for dietary needs, like suggesting gluten-free flour or vegan alternatives in the tag instructions.

Stained Glass Cookies

 24 cookies   10 minutes

Calories per Serving: 150 kcal
Proteins: 2g
Fats: 6g
Carbs: 22g

INGREDIENTS

2 1/2 cups all-purpose flour (300g)
1/2 cup granulated sugar (100g)
1 cup unsalted butter, softened (230g)
1 large egg
1 teaspoon vanilla extract (5ml)
1/4 teaspoon salt
1/4 teaspoon ground cinnamon (optional)
1/2 teaspoon baking powder (2.5g)
Assorted hard candies (such as Jolly Ranchers or lifesavers), crushed

NOTES

These cookies can be stored in an airtight container for up to a week, making them a convenient option for preparing ahead of time.

Experiment with different hard candy colors to create a vibrant assortment of stained-glass effects.

For an extra festive twist, add a bit of edible glitter or shimmer to the cookie dough before baking.

DIRECTIONS

1. Preheat the oven to 350°F (180°C). Line two baking sheets with parchment paper.
2. In a large bowl, cream together the butter and sugar until light and fluffy. Beat in the egg and vanilla extract.
3. In another bowl, whisk together the flour, salt, baking powder, and cinnamon (if using).
4. Gradually add the dry ingredients to the wet mixture, stirring until a dough forms.
5. Roll the dough out on a lightly floured surface to about 1/4-inch thickness. Use holiday-themed cookie cutters to cut out shapes (stars, trees, snowflakes), then use a smaller cutter or the tip of a knife to cut out a smaller shape in the center of each cookie.
6. Transfer the cookies to the prepared baking sheets and fill the center holes with the crushed hard candies, spreading them evenly within the cutouts.
7. Bake for 10-12 minutes, or until the cookies are lightly golden at the edges and the candy has melted into a stained glass effect.
8. Let the cookies cool on the baking sheet for a few minutes before transferring to a wire rack to cool completely.

Peppermint Bark

🍴 24 cookies   🕐 20 minutes

Calories per Serving: 160 kcal
Proteins: 2g
Fats: 9g
Carbs: 20g

INGREDIENTS

1 312 oz semi-sweet or dark chocolate (340g), chopped
12 oz white chocolate (340g), chopped
1/2 teaspoon peppermint extract
1/2 cup crushed peppermint candies or candy canes (about 4 large candy canes)

DIRECTIONS

1. Melt the semi-sweet or dark chocolate: In a heatproof bowl, melt the semi-sweet or dark chocolate in the microwave in 30-second intervals, stirring until smooth. Alternatively, melt using a double boiler.
2. Spread the chocolate: Line a baking sheet with parchment paper. Pour the melted dark chocolate onto the sheet and spread into an even layer about 1/4 inch thick. Refrigerate for 10-15 minutes until firm.
3. Melt the white chocolate: Melt the white chocolate using the same method. Stir in the peppermint extract.
4. Spread the white chocolate: Pour the melted white chocolate over the set dark chocolate layer and spread evenly.
5. Add the peppermint: Immediately sprinkle the crushed peppermint candies or candy canes over the top, pressing lightly so they adhere.
6. Chill and break: Refrigerate the bark for about 30 minutes, or until fully set. Once firm, break it into bite-sized pieces for serving or gifting.

NOTES

Peppermint bark can be stored in an airtight container at room temperature or in the refrigerator for up to 2 weeks.
To make the bark more festive, use colored candy canes (red and green) or sprinkle a little edible glitter on top for a sparkly finish.
For a more intense peppermint flavor, increase the amount of peppermint extract in the white chocolate layer.

Almond Snowball Cookies

 24 cookies 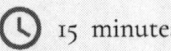 15 minutes

Calories per Serving: 130 kcal
Proteins: 2g
Fats: 8g
Carbs: 14g

INGREDIENTS

1 cup unsalted butter, softened (230g)
1/2 cup powdered sugar (60g) (plus extra for rolling)
1 teaspoon vanilla extract (5ml)
2 cups all-purpose flour (240g)
1 cup finely chopped almonds (120g)
1/4 teaspoon salt

DIRECTIONS

1. Preheat the oven to 350°F (180°C). Line a baking sheet with parchment paper.
2. In a large bowl, cream the butter and powdered sugar until light and fluffy. Add the vanilla extract and mix well.
3. Gradually add the flour, salt, and finely chopped almonds, stirring until a soft dough forms.
4. Roll the dough into 1-inch balls and place them on the prepared baking sheet about 2 inches apart.
5. Bake for 12-15 minutes, or until the cookies are lightly golden on the bottom.
6. Remove from the oven and let the cookies cool for 5 minutes. While still warm, roll them in powdered sugar to coat.
7. Once completely cooled, roll the cookies in powdered sugar again for a thicker coating.

NOTES

These cookies store well in an airtight container for up to a week, making them perfect for gifting.
You can substitute almonds with other nuts like pecans or walnuts for a variation in flavor.
Roll the cookies in powdered sugar twice to ensure they have that classic snowball appearance.

Holiday Thumbprint Cookies

24 cookies   15 minutes

Calories per Serving: 110 kcal
Proteins: 2g
Fats: 6g
Carbs: 14g

INGREDIENTS

1 cup unsalted butter, softened (230g)
1/2 cup granulated sugar (100g)
2 cups all-purpose flour (240g)
1/2 teaspoon vanilla extract (2.5ml)
1/4 teaspoon salt
1/2 cup jam or preserves (raspberry, strawberry, or apricot)

DIRECTIONS

1. Preheat the oven to 350°F (180°C). Line a baking sheet with parchment paper.
2. In a large bowl, cream together the butter and sugar until light and fluffy. Add the vanilla extract and mix well.
3. Gradually add the flour and salt, mixing until a soft dough forms.
4. Roll the dough into 1-inch balls and place them on the prepared baking sheet about 2 inches apart.
5. Use your thumb or the back of a spoon to make a small indentation in the center of each cookie.
6. Fill each indentation with a small spoonful of jam or preserves.
7. Bake for 12-15 minutes, or until the edges are lightly golden. Let the cookies cool on the baking sheet for a few minutes before transferring to a wire rack to cool completely.

NOTES

These cookies can be stored in an airtight container at room temperature for up to a week.
You can use different flavors of jam to offer a variety of colors and tastes. Try mixing apricot, raspberry, and strawberry for a colorful gift.
Dust the cookies lightly with powdered sugar for an extra festive touch before packaging.

Chapter 2: Festive Cakes, Pies & Tarts

The holiday season brings with it an opportunity to create warm, indulgent desserts that everyone loves. In this chapter, you'll find a range of festive cakes, pies, and tarts that capture the essence of Christmas. From traditional fruitcakes and Yule Logs to spiced tarts and flavorful pies, each recipe is designed to add a touch of holiday magic to your table. Whether you're baking for family gatherings or giving edible gifts, these show-stopping desserts will be the perfect centerpiece for your holiday celebrations.

Rich Fruitcake

🍴 12-16 slices   🕐 2 1/2 to 3 hours

Calories per Serving: 350 kcal
Proteins: 5g
Fats: 12g
Carbs: 55g

INGREDIENTS

1 cup unsalted butter, softened (230g)
1 cup brown sugar, packed (200g)
4 large eggs
2 cups all-purpose flour (240g)
1 teaspoon baking powder
1 teaspoon ground cinnamon
1/2 teaspoon ground nutmeg
1/4 teaspoon ground cloves
1/4 cup brandy or rum (60ml)
1 cup chopped almonds or walnuts (120g)
2 cups mixed dried fruit (such as raisins, currants, chopped dates, and apricots) (300g)
1/2 cup candied orange peel (80g)
1/2 cup candied cherries, chopped (80g)
Zest of 1 lemon and 1 orange

NOTES

Fruitcakes can be stored for several weeks and even months if kept properly wrapped and in a cool, dark place.
Feel free to swap out some of the dried fruits and nuts to suit personal preferences, such as using figs, cranberries, or hazelnuts.

DIRECTIONS

1. Prepare the oven: Preheat the oven to 300°F (150°C). Grease and line an 8-inch round cake pan with parchment paper.
2. Cream the butter and sugar: In a large bowl, cream the butter and sugar until light and fluffy. Add the eggs, one at a time, mixing well after each addition.
3. Mix the dry ingredients: In a separate bowl, sift together the flour, baking powder, cinnamon, nutmeg, and cloves.
4. Combine the wet and dry ingredients: Gradually fold the dry ingredients into the creamed butter and sugar mixture. Stir in the brandy or rum.
5. Add the fruits and nuts: Stir in the chopped nuts, dried fruits, candied peel, cherries, and zest until evenly distributed.
6. Bake the cake: Pour the batter into the prepared cake pan and smooth the top. Bake for 2 1/2 to 3 hours, or until a skewer inserted into the center comes out clean.
7. Cool and store: Let the cake cool in the pan for 10 minutes before transferring to a wire rack to cool completely. Once cooled, wrap the cake in plastic wrap and foil, and store in a cool, dark place. For the best flavor, let the cake mature for at least a week before serving.

German Stollen

 12-16 slices   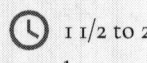 1 1/2 to 2 hours

Calories per Serving: 300 kcal
Proteins: 6g
Fats: 10g
Carbs: 45g

INGREDIENTS

4 cups all-purpose flour (480g)
1/2 cup granulated sugar (100g)
1/2 teaspoon salt
1 packet active dry yeast (7g)
1 cup whole milk, warm (240ml)
1/2 cup unsalted butter, melted (115g)
1 large egg
1 teaspoon vanilla extract (5ml)
1/2 teaspoon ground cinnamon
1/4 teaspoon ground nutmeg
1 cup mixed dried fruit (such as raisins, currants, and chopped apricots) (150g)
1/2 cup candied orange and lemon peel (80g)
1/2 cup chopped almonds (60g)
1/4 cup rum or brandy (60ml)
Powdered sugar, for dusting
Marzipan (optional, for filling)

NOTES

Stollen can be stored for up to a few weeks if wrapped tightly in foil and kept in a cool, dry place. The flavors deepen as the loaf ages.
You can customize the filling by adding different dried fruits, nuts, or even using a marzipan alternative.

DIRECTIONS

1. Soak the fruits: In a small bowl, soak the mixed dried fruit, candied peel, and chopped almonds in the rum or brandy for at least 1 hour, or overnight for a richer flavor.
2. Prepare the dough: In a large mixing bowl, combine the flour, sugar, salt, and yeast. In another bowl, whisk together the warm milk, melted butter, egg, vanilla extract, cinnamon, and nutmeg.
3. Mix and knead: Gradually add the wet ingredients to the dry ingredients, mixing until a dough forms. Knead the dough on a floured surface for 5-7 minutes, or until smooth and elastic.
4. Incorporate the fruit: Drain the soaked fruits and gently knead them into the dough until evenly distributed. Cover the dough and let it rise in a warm place for 1 to 1 1/2 hours, or until doubled in size.
5. Shape the Stollen: Preheat the oven to 350°F (180°C). Roll the dough out into a rectangle, about 1/2 inch thick. If using marzipan, roll it into a log and place it in the center of the dough. Fold the dough over the marzipan and shape it into a loaf.
6. Bake: Transfer the loaf to a parchment-lined baking sheet and bake for 1 1/2 to 2 hours, or until golden brown and a skewer inserted into the center comes out clean.
7. Dust with powdered sugar: While the Stollen is still warm, generously dust it with powdered sugar. Let it cool completely before slicing.

Italian Panettone

🍴 10-12 slices   🕒 50 minutes

Calories per Serving: 270 kcal
Proteins: 7g
Fats: 12g
Carbs: 35g

INGREDIENTS

For the dough:
- 3 1/2 cups all-purpose flour (420g)
- 1/2 cup granulated sugar (100g)
- 1 packet active dry yeast (7g)
- 1/2 cup warm milk (120ml)
- 1/2 cup unsalted butter, softened (115g)
- 3 large eggs, plus 1 egg yolk
- 1 teaspoon vanilla extract (5ml)
- Zest of 1 lemon
- Zest of 1 orange
- 1/2 teaspoon salt

For the filling:
- 1/2 cup raisins (75g)
- 1/2 cup candied orange peel (75g)
- 1/4 cup dried cranberries (optional)
- 1/4 cup rum or warm water (60ml) (to soak the raisins)

NOTES

Panettone can be stored at room temperature for up to a week, making it a great make-ahead gift.
If you don't have a special panettone mold, a tall cake pan or even a cleaned-out coffee tin can be used.

DIRECTIONS

1. Soak the raisins: In a small bowl, soak the raisins in rum (or warm water) for at least 30 minutes. Drain before adding to the dough.
2. Prepare the dough: In a small bowl, dissolve the yeast in the warm milk and let it sit for 5-10 minutes until frothy. In a large mixing bowl, combine the flour, sugar, lemon and orange zest, and salt.
3. Mix the wet ingredients: In a separate bowl, whisk together the eggs, egg yolk, vanilla extract, and softened butter.
4. Combine and knead: Add the yeast mixture and the wet ingredients to the dry ingredients. Stir until a sticky dough forms. Knead the dough on a floured surface for 5-7 minutes, until smooth and elastic.
5. Add the fruit: Gently knead the soaked raisins, candied orange peel, and cranberries into the dough until evenly distributed.
6. Let the dough rise: Shape the dough into a ball and place it in a greased bowl. Cover with a damp cloth and let it rise in a warm place for 1 1/2 to 2 hours, or until doubled in size.
7. Second rise in the pan: Punch down the dough and place it in a greased and floured panettone mold or a tall, round baking tin. Let it rise again for 45-60 minutes.
8. Bake the panettone: Preheat the oven to 350°F (180°C). Bake the panettone for 45-50 minutes, or until golden brown on top and a skewer inserted in the center comes out clean.
9. Cool and serve: Let the panettone cool before slicing and serving.

Yule Log (Bûche de Noël)

🍴 10-12 slices 🕐 15 minutes

Calories per Serving: 280 kcal
Proteins: 5g
Fats: 14g
Carbs: 35g

INGREDIENTS

For the sponge cake:

1 cup all-purpose flour (120g)
1/4 cup unsweetened cocoa powder (25g)
1 teaspoon baking powder
1/4 teaspoon salt
4 large eggs
3/4 cup granulated sugar (150g)
1 teaspoon vanilla extract (5ml)
Powdered sugar (for dusting)

For the filling:

1 1/2 cups heavy cream (360ml)
2 tablespoons powdered sugar (30g)
1 teaspoon vanilla extract (5ml)

For the chocolate ganache (for the frosting):

1 cup semi-sweet chocolate (175g), chopped
1/2 cup heavy cream (120ml)

NOTES

The Yule Log can be made a day in advance and stored in the fridge, covered, to allow the flavors to develop.

Feel free to decorate the log with meringue mushrooms or marzipan holly leaves for an extra festive touch.

DIRECTIONS

1. Preheat the oven: Set the oven to 350°F (175°C). Line a 10x15-inch jelly roll pan with parchment paper and grease it lightly.
2. Make the sponge cake: In a bowl, sift together the flour, cocoa powder, baking powder, and salt. In a separate bowl, beat the eggs and sugar with an electric mixer until pale and thick. Stir in the vanilla extract.
3. Combine and bake: Gently fold the dry ingredients into the wet mixture until just combined. Pour the batter into the prepared pan and spread it evenly. Bake for 12-15 minutes, or until the cake springs back when touched.
4. Roll the cake: While the cake is still warm, dust a clean kitchen towel with powdered sugar. Invert the cake onto the towel, peel off the parchment paper, and roll the cake up (with the towel inside) starting from one short end. Let it cool completely in the rolled shape.
5. Make the filling: In a bowl, whip the heavy cream, powdered sugar, and vanilla extract until stiff peaks form.
6. Fill the cake: Once the cake has cooled, unroll it gently and spread the whipped cream filling evenly over the surface. Roll the cake back up (without the towel).
7. Prepare the ganache: Heat the heavy cream until just simmering and pour it over the chopped chocolate. Let it sit for a minute, then stir until smooth.
8. Frost the cake: Spread the ganache over the rolled cake to resemble tree bark. Use a fork to create a bark-like texture. Dust with powdered sugar to resemble snow.

Pumpkin Spice Cake

🍴 12-16 slices   🕐 40 minutes

Calories per Serving: 320 kcal
Proteins: 4g
Fats: 15g
Carbs: 45g

INGREDIENTS

2 1/2 cups all-purpose flour (300g)

1 cup granulated sugar (200g)

1/2 cup brown sugar, packed (100g)

1 teaspoon baking soda

1 teaspoon baking powder

2 teaspoons ground cinnamon

1 teaspoon ground nutmeg

1/2 teaspoon ground ginger

1/4 teaspoon ground cloves

1/2 teaspoon salt

1 cup canned pumpkin purée (240g)

1/2 cup vegetable oil (120ml)

1/2 cup unsweetened applesauce (120ml)

4 large eggs

1 teaspoon vanilla extract (5ml)

DIRECTIONS

1. Preheat the oven: Set the oven to 350°F (175°C). Grease and flour a 9x13-inch baking pan.
2. Combine dry ingredients: In a large bowl, whisk together the flour, baking soda, baking powder, cinnamon, nutmeg, ginger, cloves, and salt.
3. Mix wet ingredients: In another bowl, whisk together the sugar, brown sugar, pumpkin purée, vegetable oil, applesauce, eggs, and vanilla extract until smooth.
4. Combine and mix: Gradually fold the wet ingredients into the dry ingredients until just combined, being careful not to overmix.
5. Bake the cake: Pour the batter into the prepared pan and bake for 35-40 minutes, or until a toothpick inserted into the center comes out clean.
6. Cool and serve: Let the cake cool completely in the pan before frosting or serving.

Optional Cream Cheese Frosting:
1. 8 oz cream cheese, softened (230g)
2. 1/4 cup unsalted butter, softened (60g)
3. 2 cups powdered sugar (240g)
4. 1 teaspoon vanilla extract (5ml)

Instructions for Frosting:
1. In a large bowl, beat together the cream cheese and butter until light and fluffy.
2. Gradually add the powdered sugar, beating until smooth.
3. Stir in the vanilla extract and spread the frosting over the cooled cake.

NOTES

Fruitcakes can be stored for several weeks and even months if kept properly wrapped and in a cool, dark place.

Feel free to swap out some of the dried fruits and nuts to suit personal preferences, such as using figs, cranberries, or hazelnuts.

Gingerbread Cake with Cream Cheese Frosting

12-16 slices   40 minutes

Calories per Serving: 320 kcal
Proteins: 4g
Fats: 15g
Carbs: 45g

INGREDIENTS

Ingredients for the Cake:
- 2 1/2 cups all-purpose flour (300g)
- 1 cup brown sugar, packed (200g)
- 1/2 cup molasses (120ml)
- 1/2 cup unsalted butter, softened (115g)
- 2 large eggs
- 1 cup buttermilk (240ml)
- 2 teaspoons ground ginger
- 2 teaspoons ground cinnamon
- 1/4 teaspoon ground cloves
- 1/4 teaspoon ground nutmeg
- 1 teaspoon baking soda
- 1/2 teaspoon baking powder
- 1/2 teaspoon salt

Ingredients for the Cream Cheese Frosting:
- 8 oz cream cheese, softened (230g)
- 1/4 cup unsalted butter, softened (60g)
- 2 cups powdered sugar (240g)
- 1 teaspoon vanilla extract (5ml)

NOTES

The cake can be stored in the refrigerator for up to a week, covered tightly.
For an extra festive touch, top the frosted cake with a sprinkle of cinnamon or gingerbread cookie crumbles.

DIRECTIONS

1. Preheat the oven: Set the oven to 350°F (175°C). Grease and flour a 9x13-inch baking pan.
2. Make the cake batter: In a large bowl, cream together the butter and brown sugar until light and fluffy. Beat in the eggs one at a time, followed by the molasses and buttermilk.
3. Combine dry ingredients: In a separate bowl, whisk together the flour, baking soda, baking powder, spices, and salt.
4. Mix wet and dry: Gradually fold the dry ingredients into the wet mixture until just combined, being careful not to overmix.
5. Bake the cake: Pour the batter into the prepared pan and bake for 35-40 minutes, or until a toothpick inserted into the center comes out clean.
6. Cool the cake: Let the cake cool completely in the pan before frosting.

Instructions for Frosting:
1. In a large bowl, beat together the cream cheese and butter until light and fluffy.
2. Gradually add the powdered sugar and beat until smooth.
3. Stir in the vanilla extract and spread the frosting over the cooled gingerbread cake.

Eggnog Cupcakes

🍴 12 cupcakes   🕐 20 minutes

Calories per Serving: 280 kcal
Proteins: 4g
Fats: 12g
Carbs: 38g

INGREDIENTS

Ingredients for the Cupcakes:
1 1/4 cups all-purpose flour (150g)
1 teaspoon baking powder
1/4 teaspoon salt
1/2 teaspoon ground nutmeg
1/4 teaspoon ground cinnamon
1/2 cup unsalted butter, softened (115g)
3/4 cup granulated sugar (150g)
2 large eggs
1/2 teaspoon vanilla extract (2.5ml)
1/2 cup eggnog (120ml)

Ingredients for the Frosting:
1/2 cup unsalted butter, softened (115g)
2 cups powdered sugar (240g)
2 tablespoons eggnog (30ml)
1/2 teaspoon vanilla extract (2.5ml)
Ground nutmeg for sprinkling

NOTES

You can store the cupcakes in an airtight container in the fridge for up to 3 days. For a boozy twist, add a tablespoon of rum to the cupcake batter and the frosting.

DIRECTIONS

1. Preheat the oven: Set the oven to 350°F (175°C) and line a 12-cup muffin pan with cupcake liners.
2. Mix dry ingredients: In a bowl, whisk together the flour, baking powder, salt, nutmeg, and cinnamon.
3. Cream butter and sugar: In another bowl, beat the butter and sugar together until light and fluffy. Add the eggs one at a time, mixing well after each addition. Stir in the vanilla extract.
4. Combine wet and dry ingredients: Gradually add the dry ingredients to the butter mixture, alternating with the eggnog, beginning and ending with the dry ingredients. Mix until just combined.
5. Bake: Divide the batter evenly among the cupcake liners and bake for 18-20 minutes, or until a toothpick inserted into the center comes out clean. Let the cupcakes cool completely on a wire rack before frosting.
6. Frosting Instructions:
7. Beat butter and sugar: In a bowl, beat the softened butter until creamy. Gradually add the powdered sugar and continue beating until smooth.
8. Add eggnog and vanilla: Beat in the eggnog and vanilla extract until the frosting is light and fluffy.
9. Frost the cupcakes: Once the cupcakes have cooled, frost them with the eggnog frosting and sprinkle with ground nutmeg for a festive touch.

Peppermint Mocha Cupcakes

🍴 12 cupcakes   🕐 20 minutes

Calories per Serving: 300 kcal
Proteins: 4g
Fats: 14g
Carbs: 38g

NOTES

The cake can be stored in the refrigerator for up to a week, covered tightly.

For an extra festive touch, top the frosted cake with a sprinkle of cinnamon or gingerbread cookie crumbles.

INGREDIENTS

1 1/4 cups all-purpose flour (150g)
1/4 cup unsweetened cocoa powder (25g)
1 teaspoon baking powder
1/2 teaspoon baking soda
1/4 teaspoon salt
1/2 cup unsalted butter, softened (115g)
3/4 cup granulated sugar (150g)
2 large eggs
1/2 teaspoon vanilla extract (2.5ml)
1/2 teaspoon peppermint extract (2.5ml)
1/2 cup brewed coffee, cooled (120ml)
1/4 cup milk (60ml)

Ingredients for the Frosting:
1/2 cup unsalted butter, softened (115g)
2 cups powdered sugar (240g)
2 tablespoons unsweetened cocoa powder (15g)
2 tablespoons brewed coffee, cooled (30ml)
1/2 teaspoon peppermint extract (2.5ml)
Crushed candy canes for topping (optional)

DIRECTIONS

1. Preheat the oven: Set the oven to 350°F (175°C) and line a 12-cup muffin pan with cupcake liners.
2. Combine dry ingredients: In a bowl, whisk together the flour, cocoa powder, baking powder, baking soda, and salt.
3. Cream butter and sugar: In a separate bowl, beat the butter and sugar until light and fluffy. Add the eggs, one at a time, beating well after each addition. Stir in the vanilla and peppermint extracts.
4. Alternate wet and dry: Gradually add the dry ingredients to the butter mixture, alternating with the brewed coffee and milk, beginning and ending with the dry ingredients. Mix until just combined.
5. Bake: Divide the batter evenly among the cupcake liners and bake for 18-20 minutes, or until a toothpick inserted into the center comes out clean. Allow the cupcakes to cool completely before frosting.

Frosting Instructions:

1. Prepare the frosting: Beat the butter until creamy, then gradually add the powdered sugar and cocoa powder. Slowly beat in the brewed coffee and peppermint extract until the frosting is light and fluffy.
2. Frost and decorate: Frost the cooled cupcakes and sprinkle with crushed candy canes for a festive touch.

Mulled Wine Cupcakes

🍴 12 cupcakes   🕐 20 minutes

Calories per Serving: 310 kcal
Proteins: 4g
Fats: 12g
Carbs: 42g

NOTES

TYou can store the cupcakes in an airtight container for up to 3 days at room temperature or in the refrigerator for up to a week.

If you don't have mulled wine, you can use red wine with a bit of cinnamon, cloves, and orange zest added while warming.

INGREDIENTS

1 1/4 cups all-purpose flour (150g)
1/4 cup unsweetened cocoa powder (25g)
1 teaspoon baking powder
1/2 teaspoon baking soda
1/4 teaspoon salt
1/2 cup unsalted butter, softened (115g)
3/4 cup granulated sugar (150g)
2 large eggs
1/2 teaspoon vanilla extract (2.5ml)
1/2 teaspoon ground cinnamon
1/4 teaspoon ground cloves
1/4 teaspoon ground nutmeg
3/4 cup mulled wine, cooled (180ml)
Ingredients for the Frosting:
1/2 cup unsalted butter, softened (115g)
2 cups powdered sugar (240g)
2 tablespoons mulled wine, reduced (30ml)
Zest of 1 orange
Ground cinnamon for dusting (optional)

DIRECTIONS

1. Preheat the oven: Set the oven to 350°F (175°C) and line a 12-cup muffin pan with cupcake liners.
2. Combine dry ingredients: In a bowl, whisk together the flour, cocoa powder, baking powder, baking soda, cinnamon, cloves, nutmeg, and salt.
3. Cream butter and sugar: In a separate bowl, beat the butter and sugar until light and fluffy. Add the eggs one at a time, beating well after each addition. Stir in the vanilla extract.
4. Alternate wet and dry: Gradually add the dry ingredients to the butter mixture, alternating with the mulled wine. Mix until just combined.
5. Bake: Divide the batter evenly among the cupcake liners and bake for 18-20 minutes, or until a toothpick inserted into the center comes out clean. Allow the cupcakes to cool completely before frosting.

Frosting Instructions:

1. Prepare the frosting: Beat the softened butter until creamy. Gradually add the powdered sugar and beat until smooth. Add the reduced mulled wine and orange zest, and beat until the frosting is fluffy.
2. Frost and decorate: Frost the cooled cupcakes and dust with cinnamon for an extra festive touch.

Classic Pumpkin Pie

🍴 8 slices 🕐 60 minutes

Calories per Serving: 320 kcal
Proteins: 5g
Fats: 15g
Carbs: 42g

INGREDIENTS

For the crust:
- 1 1/4 cups all-purpose flour (150g)
- 1/2 teaspoon salt
- 1/2 cup unsalted butter, cold and cubed (115g)
- 2-4 tablespoons ice water

For the filling:
- 1 (15 oz) can pumpkin purée (425g)
- 3/4 cup granulated sugar (150g)
- 1 teaspoon ground cinnamon
- 1/2 teaspoon ground ginger
- 1/4 teaspoon ground cloves
- 2 large eggs
- 1 (12 oz) can evaporated milk (354ml)
- 1 teaspoon vanilla extract (5ml)

DIRECTIONS

1. Prepare the crust: In a large bowl, whisk together the flour and salt. Cut in the cold butter until the mixture resembles coarse crumbs. Gradually add the ice water, 1 tablespoon at a time, mixing until the dough comes together. Form into a disk, wrap in plastic, and chill for at least 30 minutes.
2. Roll out the crust: Preheat the oven to 375°F (190°C). Roll out the chilled dough on a lightly floured surface and fit it into a 9-inch pie dish. Trim and crimp the edges. Blind bake the crust by lining it with parchment paper, filling it with pie weights or beans, and baking for 10-12 minutes.
3. Make the filling: In a medium bowl, whisk together the pumpkin purée, sugar, cinnamon, ginger, and cloves. Beat in the eggs, then stir in the evaporated milk and vanilla extract until smooth.
4. Bake the pie: Pour the pumpkin mixture into the partially baked crust. Bake for 50-60 minutes, or until the center is set and a toothpick comes out clean. Allow to cool completely before serving.

NOTES

The pie can be stored in the refrigerator for up to 4 days, making it perfect for prepping ahead.

Add a dollop of whipped cream and a sprinkle of cinnamon for an extra festive touch.

Mince Pies

🍴 12 pies 🕐 25 minutes

Calories per Serving: 250 kcal
Proteins: 3g
Fats: 12g
Carbs: 32g

INGREDIENTS

For the pastry:
- 2 cups all-purpose flour (240g)
- 1/2 cup unsalted butter, cold and cubed (115g)
- 1/4 cup granulated sugar (50g)
- 1 egg yolk
- 2-3 tablespoons cold water

For the filling:
- 1 1/2 cups mincemeat (store-bought or homemade)
- Powdered sugar (for dusting)

DIRECTIONS

1. Prepare the pastry: In a large bowl, rub the butter into the flour with your fingertips until the mixture resembles breadcrumbs. Stir in the sugar. Add the egg yolk and cold water, 1 tablespoon at a time, until the dough comes together. Form into a disk, wrap in plastic, and chill for 30 minutes.
2. Preheat the oven: Set the oven to 375°F (190°C). Grease a 12-cup muffin tin.
3. Roll out the pastry: On a floured surface, roll out the chilled pastry to about 1/8 inch thick. Use a round cutter to cut out 12 circles to fit the muffin tin, then press them into the prepared tin.
4. Fill and top the pies: Spoon about 1 tablespoon of mincemeat into each pastry shell. Roll out the remaining pastry and cut out smaller rounds or festive shapes (stars, trees, etc.) for the tops.
5. Bake: Bake for 20-25 minutes, or until the pastry is golden brown. Allow the mince pies to cool in the tin for 5 minutes before transferring to a wire rack.
6. Dust and serve: Once cooled, dust the mince pies with powdered sugar before serving.

NOTES

Mincemeat is a mix of dried fruits, spices, and sometimes alcohol (like brandy). You can use store-bought mincemeat or make your own ahead of time.

These pies can be stored in an airtight container at room temperature for up to 5 days.

Pecan Pie

8 slices ⏲ 55 minutes

Calories per Serving: 500 kcal
Proteins: 6g
Fats: 27g
Carbs: 65g

INGREDIENTS

the crust:
- 1 1/4 cups all-purpose flour (150g)
- 1/2 teaspoon salt
- 1/2 cup unsalted butter, cold and cubed (115g)
- 2-4 tablespoons ice water

For the filling:
- 1 cup light corn syrup (240ml)
- 1 cup packed brown sugar (200g)
- 1/4 cup unsalted butter, melted (60g)
- 3 large eggs
- 1 teaspoon vanilla extract (5ml)
- 1/4 teaspoon salt
- 2 cups pecan halves (250g)

NOTES

Store the pie at room temperature for up to 2 days or in the fridge for up to 4 days. Serve with a dollop of whipped cream or vanilla ice cream for a rich dessert experience.

DIRECTIONS

1. Prepare the crust: In a large bowl, whisk together the flour and salt. Cut in the cold butter until the mixture resembles coarse crumbs. Gradually add ice water, 1 tablespoon at a time, until the dough forms. Shape into a disk, wrap in plastic wrap, and chill for at least 30 minutes.
2. Roll out the crust: Preheat the oven to 350°F (175°C). Roll out the chilled dough on a lightly floured surface and fit it into a 9-inch pie dish. Trim and crimp the edges.
3. Make the filling: In a medium bowl, whisk together the corn syrup, brown sugar, melted butter, eggs, vanilla extract, and salt until smooth. Stir in the pecan halves.
4. Assemble and bake: Pour the pecan mixture into the prepared pie crust. Bake for 50-55 minutes, or until the center is set. If the crust starts to brown too quickly, cover the edges with foil.
5. Cool and serve: Let the pie cool completely before slicing and serving.

Pear and Almond Tart

🍴 8-10 slices   🕐 45 minutes

Calories per Serving: 320 kcal
Proteins: 6g
Fats: 20g
Carbs: 28g

INGREDIENTS

For the tart crust:
- 1 1/4 cups all-purpose flour (150g)
- 1/2 cup unsalted butter, cold and cubed (115g)
- 1/4 cup powdered sugar (30g)
- 1 egg yolk
- 2-3 tablespoons cold water

For the almond filling (frangipane):
- 1 cup almond flour (100g)
- 1/2 cup unsalted butter, softened (115g)
- 1/2 cup granulated sugar (100g)
- 2 large eggs
- 1/2 teaspoon almond extract (2.5ml)

For the topping:
- 3 ripe pears, peeled, cored, and sliced
  - 2 tablespoons apricot jam (optional, for glazing)

NOTES

Store the pie at room temperature for up to 2 days or in the fridge for up to 4 days. Serve with a dollop of whipped cream or vanilla ice cream for a rich dessert experience.

DIRECTIONS

1. Prepare the crust: In a large bowl, combine the flour and powdered sugar. Rub in the cold butter with your fingertips until the mixture resembles breadcrumbs. Stir in the egg yolk and enough cold water to bring the dough together. Wrap the dough in plastic and chill for 30 minutes.
2. Preheat the oven: Set the oven to 375°F (190°C). Roll out the chilled dough on a lightly floured surface and fit it into a 9-inch tart pan. Trim the edges and prick the base with a fork. Line with parchment paper and fill with pie weights or beans. Bake for 10-12 minutes, then remove the weights and bake for another 5 minutes until lightly golden.
3. Make the frangipane (almond filling): In a bowl, cream together the softened butter and sugar until light and fluffy. Add the eggs one at a time, then stir in the almond flour and almond extract until combined.
4. Assemble the tart: Spread the almond filling evenly over the partially baked crust. Arrange the pear slices in a fan pattern on top of the filling.
5. Bake: Bake for 40-45 minutes, or until the filling is set and the pears are tender. If desired, brush the tart with warmed apricot jam for a glossy finish.
6. Cool and serve: Let the tart cool completely before slicing and serving.

Cranberry Orange Tart

🍴 8-10 slices   🕐 45 minutes

Calories per Serving: 280 kcal
Proteins: 5g
Fats: 15g
Carbs: 32g

INGREDIENTS

For the crust:
- 1 1/4 cups all-purpose flour (150g)
- 1/2 cup unsalted butter, cold and cubed (115g)
- 1/4 cup powdered sugar (30g)
- 1 egg yolk
- 2-3 tablespoons cold water

For the cranberry filling:
- 2 cups fresh or frozen cranberries (200g)
- 1/2 cup orange juice (120ml)
- Zest of 1 orange
- 3/4 cup granulated sugar (150g)
- 1/4 cup water (60ml)
- 2 tablespoons cornstarch (16g)

For the topping (optional):
- Whipped cream or powdered sugar for dusting

DIRECTIONS

1. **Prepare the crust:** In a large bowl, combine the flour and powdered sugar. Rub in the cold butter until the mixture resembles breadcrumbs. Stir in the egg yolk and enough cold water to bring the dough together. Wrap the dough in plastic and chill for 30 minutes.
2. **Preheat the oven:** Set the oven to 375°F (190°C). Roll out the chilled dough on a lightly floured surface and fit it into a 9-inch tart pan. Trim the edges and prick the base with a fork. Line with parchment paper and fill with pie weights or beans. Bake for 10-12 minutes, then remove the weights and bake for another 5 minutes until lightly golden.
3. **Make the cranberry filling:** In a medium saucepan, combine the cranberries, orange juice, orange zest, sugar, and water. Bring to a simmer over medium heat until the cranberries burst and the mixture thickens. Stir in the cornstarch and cook for another 2-3 minutes until the filling is smooth.
4. **Assemble the tart:** Pour the cranberry filling into the partially baked crust and spread evenly.
5. **Bake:** Bake for 25-30 minutes, or until the filling is set. Let the tart cool completely before serving.
6. **Decorate and serve:** Dust with powdered sugar or serve with whipped cream.

NOTES

This tart can be made a day ahead and stored in the refrigerator. Bring it to room temperature before serving.
The tart pairs beautifully with whipped cream or vanilla ice cream.

Pavlova with Winter Fruits

🍴 8   🕐 75 minutes

Calories per Serving: 200 kcal
Proteins: 4g
Fats: 5g
Carbs: 35g

INGREDIENTS

For the Pavlova:
- 4 large egg whites
- 1 cup granulated sugar (200g)
- 1 teaspoon cornstarch (5g)
- 1 teaspoon white vinegar (5ml)
- 1/2 teaspoon vanilla extract (2.5ml)

For the topping:
- 1 cup heavy cream, whipped (240ml)
- 1/4 cup powdered sugar (30g)
- Assorted winter fruits: pomegranate seeds, kiwi slices, orange segments, and cranberries
- A drizzle of honey (optional)
- Fresh mint leaves (optional)

DIRECTIONS

1. Preheat the oven: Set the oven to 275°F (135°C). Line a baking sheet with parchment paper and draw an 8-inch circle on the parchment as a guide.
2. Make the meringue: In a large, clean bowl, whisk the egg whites on medium speed until soft peaks form. Gradually add the granulated sugar, one tablespoon at a time, beating until stiff and glossy peaks form. Fold in the cornstarch, vinegar, and vanilla extract.
3. Shape the Pavlova: Spoon the meringue onto the parchment paper, spreading it within the circle and creating a slight dip in the center for the toppings.
4. Bake: Bake the meringue for 1 hour and 15 minutes. Turn off the oven and let the Pavlova cool inside the oven with the door slightly open to avoid cracks.
5. Assemble the Pavlova: Once the meringue has cooled, top it with whipped cream. Arrange the winter fruits—pomegranate seeds, kiwi slices, orange segments, and cranberries—on top. Drizzle with honey and garnish with fresh mint leaves if desired.

NOTES

The Pavlova can be made a day in advance, but it should be topped with cream and fruits just before serving to keep the meringue crisp.

Feel free to swap out the winter fruits for whatever seasonal fruits are available, such as persimmons, pears, or even figs.

Christmas Cheesecake

12-16 slices | 60 minutes

Calories per Serving: 400 kcal
Proteins: 7g
Fats: 30g
Carbs: 35g

INGREDIENTS

For the crust:
- 1 1/2 cups graham cracker crumbs (150g)
- 1/4 cup granulated sugar (50g)
- 1/2 cup unsalted butter, melted (115g)

For the cheesecake filling:
- 24 oz cream cheese, softened (680g)
- 1 cup granulated sugar (200g)
- 1 teaspoon vanilla extract (5ml)
- 3 large eggs
- 1/2 cup sour cream (120ml)
- 1/4 cup heavy cream (60ml)

For the topping:
- Whipped cream
- Red and green sprinkles or crushed candy canes for decoration

NOTES
Cheesecake can be made 1-2 days in advance and stored in the refrigerator, making it a great make-ahead dessert.
Customize the toppings with other festive decorations like edible glitter or Christmas-themed chocolate pieces.

DIRECTIONS

1. Prepare the crust: Preheat the oven to 325°F (160°C). In a medium bowl, mix together the graham cracker crumbs, melted butter, and sugar. Press the mixture firmly into the bottom of a 9-inch springform pan. Bake for 8-10 minutes, then set aside to cool.

2. Make the filling: In a large bowl, beat the softened cream cheese and sugar until smooth and creamy. Add the vanilla extract, then the eggs one at a time, beating well after each addition. Mix in the sour cream and heavy cream until combined.

3. Bake the cheesecake: Pour the filling into the cooled crust. Place the springform pan in a larger pan filled with about an inch of hot water (to prevent cracking). Bake for 55-65 minutes, or until the center is slightly jiggly. Turn off the oven and leave the cheesecake inside with the door slightly open for 1 hour. Then refrigerate for at least 4 hours or overnight.

4. Decorate: Top with whipped cream and festive red and green sprinkles or crushed candy canes for a holiday touch.

Chapter 3: Savory Bakes for the Holiday Table

The holiday season isn't just about sweet treats—it's also a time to gather around the table for delicious, hearty meals. This chapter is dedicated to savory bakes that will elevate your holiday spread and bring warmth to every occasion. From flaky pies filled with seasonal vegetables to golden breads perfect for dipping into rich soups, these savory recipes are sure to impress guests and add a comforting, festive touch to your holiday table. Whether you're preparing for an intimate family dinner or hosting a grand feast, these savory bakes will become cherished favorites, balancing the sweetness of the season with delightful flavors..

Spinach and Feta Pie

🍴 8   🕒 45 minutes

Calories per Serving: 280 kcal
Proteins: 9g
Fats: 18g
Carbs: 22g

INGREDIENTS

For the filling:
- 1 lb fresh spinach, washed and chopped (450g) (or 10 oz frozen spinach, thawed and drained)
- 1 1/2 cups crumbled feta cheese (225g)
- 1/2 cup ricotta cheese (120g) (optional for a creamier texture)
- 1 medium onion, finely chopped
- 2 garlic cloves, minced
- 2 tablespoons olive oil
- 2 large eggs, beaten
- 1/4 teaspoon ground nutmeg
- Salt and pepper to taste

For the crust:
- 8-10 sheets phyllo pastry (or puff pastry if preferred)
- 1/4 cup melted butter (or olive oil for brushing)

NOTES
You can add fresh herbs like dill or parsley to the filling for extra flavor.
The pie can be stored in the refrigerator for up to 3 days and reheated before serving.

DIRECTIONS

1. Preheat the oven: Set the oven to 350°F (175°C).
2. Cook the spinach: In a large pan, heat the olive oil over medium heat. Sauté the chopped onion and garlic until soft and fragrant, about 3-5 minutes. Add the spinach and cook until wilted (if using fresh spinach) or until heated through (if using frozen spinach). Remove from heat and let it cool slightly.
3. Make the filling: In a large bowl, combine the cooked spinach mixture, crumbled feta, ricotta (if using), beaten eggs, and nutmeg. Season with salt and pepper.
4. Prepare the phyllo crust: Grease a 9-inch pie dish or baking pan. Lay a sheet of phyllo pastry in the dish, letting the edges hang over the sides. Brush with melted butter or olive oil. Layer 8-10 sheets, brushing each layer with butter or oil.
5. Add the filling: Spoon the spinach and feta filling into the prepared crust. Fold over the excess phyllo dough and brush the top with more melted butter.
6. Bake: Bake for 40-45 minutes, or until the phyllo is golden brown and crisp. Allow to cool for 10 minutes before slicing and serving.

Mushroom and Goat Cheese Tart

8 | 45 minutes

Calories per Serving: 290 kcal
Proteins: 8g
Fats: 22g
Carbs: 20g

INGREDIENTS

the crust:
- 1 1/4 cups all-purpose flour (150g)
- 1/2 cup unsalted butter, cold and cubed (115g)
- 1/4 cup cold water (60ml)
- 1/4 teaspoon salt

For the filling:
- 2 tablespoons olive oil
- 1 medium onion, finely chopped
- 2 garlic cloves, minced
- 1 lb mushrooms, sliced (450g) (a mix of cremini, button, or shiitake works well)
- 1 tablespoon fresh thyme or 1 teaspoon dried thyme
- 4 oz goat cheese, crumbled (120g)
- 1/2 cup heavy cream (120ml)
- 2 large eggs
- Salt and pepper to taste

NOTES
You can add a sprinkle of fresh herbs like parsley or chives for extra flavor and garnish before serving.
The tart can be stored in the refrigerator for up to 3 days and reheated in the oven before serving.

DIRECTIONS

1. Prepare the crust: In a large bowl, combine the flour and salt. Rub in the cold butter until the mixture resembles coarse crumbs. Gradually add cold water, 1 tablespoon at a time, until the dough forms. Shape into a disk, wrap in plastic, and chill for at least 30 minutes.
2. Preheat the oven: Set the oven to 375°F (190°C). Roll out the chilled dough on a floured surface and fit it into a 9-inch tart pan. Trim the edges and prick the base with a fork. Line with parchment paper and fill with pie weights or beans. Blind bake for 10-12 minutes, then remove the weights and bake for another 5 minutes.
3. Cook the mushrooms: Heat olive oil in a large skillet over medium heat. Add the chopped onion and garlic, sautéing for about 5 minutes until softened. Add the mushrooms and thyme, and cook until the mushrooms are tender and have released their moisture, about 7-10 minutes. Season with salt and pepper. Set aside to cool slightly.
4. Make the filling: In a bowl, whisk together the eggs, heavy cream, and a pinch of salt and pepper. Add the cooked mushrooms and crumbled goat cheese, stirring gently to combine.
5. Assemble and bake: Pour the filling into the pre-baked crust. Bake for 30-35 minutes, or until the tart is golden and the center is set. Let cool for 10 minutes before slicing and serving.

Bacon and Leek Quiche

🍴 8   🕒 45 minutes

Calories per Serving: 350 kcal
Proteins: 13g
Fats: 25g
Carbs: 20g

INGREDIENTS

For the crust:
- 1 1/4 cups all-purpose flour (150g)
- 1/2 cup unsalted butter, cold and cubed (115g)
- 1/4 cup cold water (60ml)
- 1/4 teaspoon salt

For the filling:
- 6 slices of bacon, cooked and crumbled
- 2 medium leeks, white and light green parts only, thinly sliced
- 1 tablespoon olive oil
- 4 large eggs
- 1 cup heavy cream (240ml)
- 1/2 cup whole milk (120ml)
- 1 cup shredded Gruyère or Swiss cheese (120g)
- Salt and pepper to taste
- A pinch of ground nutmeg (optional)

NOTES

You can store the quiche in the refrigerator for up to 3 days and reheat it before serving. Feel free to add other vegetables or swap the Gruyère for cheddar or another favorite cheese.

DIRECTIONS

1. Prepare the crust: In a large bowl, mix the flour and salt. Rub in the cold butter until the mixture resembles coarse crumbs. Gradually add cold water, 1 tablespoon at a time, until the dough forms. Shape into a disk, wrap in plastic, and chill for at least 30 minutes.

2. Preheat the oven: Set the oven to 375°F (190°C). Roll out the chilled dough on a floured surface and fit it into a 9-inch pie dish. Trim the edges and prick the base with a fork. Line with parchment paper and fill with pie weights or beans. Blind bake for 10-12 minutes, then remove the weights and bake for another 5 minutes.

3. Cook the leeks and bacon: Heat olive oil in a skillet over medium heat. Add the sliced leeks and sauté for 5-7 minutes, or until soft and fragrant. Set aside to cool slightly. Cook the bacon until crispy, then crumble and set aside.

4. Make the filling: In a large bowl, whisk together the eggs, heavy cream, and milk. Season with salt, pepper, and a pinch of nutmeg (if using). Stir in the cooked leeks, bacon, and shredded Gruyère cheese.

5. Assemble and bake: Pour the filling into the pre-baked crust. Bake for 30-35 minutes, or until the quiche is golden brown and the center is set. Let cool for 10 minutes before slicing and serving.

Roasted Vegetable and Gruyère Quiche

8 | 45 minutes

Calories per Serving: 330 kcal
Proteins: 11g
Fats: 23g
Carbs: 20g

INGREDIENTS

For the crust:
- 1 1/4 cups all-purpose flour (150g)
- 1/2 cup unsalted butter, cold and cubed (115g)
- 1/4 cup cold water (60ml)
- 1/4 teaspoon salt

For the filling:
- 1 red bell pepper, sliced
- 1 zucchini, sliced
- 1 small red onion, sliced
- 1 tablespoon olive oil
- 1 cup shredded Gruyère cheese (120g)
- 4 large eggs
- 1 cup heavy cream (240ml)
- Salt and pepper to taste
- A pinch of dried thyme or rosemary (optional)

DIRECTIONS

1. Prepare the crust: In a large bowl, combine the flour and salt. Rub in the cold butter with your fingers until the mixture resembles coarse crumbs. Add cold water, 1 tablespoon at a time, until the dough comes together. Form the dough into a disk, wrap in plastic, and chill for at least 30 minutes.
2. Preheat the oven: Set the oven to 400°F (200°C). Toss the sliced bell pepper, zucchini, and red onion with olive oil, salt, and pepper. Spread the vegetables on a baking sheet and roast for 20-25 minutes, or until tender and slightly caramelized. Remove from the oven and reduce the oven temperature to 375°F (190°C).
3. Prepare the crust: Roll out the chilled dough on a floured surface and fit it into a 9-inch tart or pie pan. Trim the edges and prick the base with a fork. Line with parchment paper and fill with pie weights or beans. Blind bake the crust for 10-12 minutes, then remove the weights and bake for another 5 minutes.
4. Make the filling: In a bowl, whisk together the eggs, heavy cream, salt, pepper, and thyme or rosemary (if using). Stir in the roasted vegetables and shredded Gruyère cheese.
5. Assemble and bake: Pour the filling into the pre-baked crust. Bake for 30-35 minutes, or until the quiche is golden and set in the center. Let cool for 10 minutes before slicing and serving.

NOTES

The quiche can be stored in the refrigerator for up to 3 days and reheated before serving. Swap out the vegetables for seasonal options like mushrooms, asparagus, or butternut squash.

Parmesan Herb Knots

12 knots   15 minutes

Calories per Serving: 150 kcal
Proteins: 4g
Fats: 8g
Carbs: 16g

INGREDIENTS

For the dough:

- 2 1/4 teaspoons active dry yeast (1 packet)
- 1 cup warm water (240ml)
- 2 1/2 cups all-purpose flour (300g)
- 1 tablespoon granulated sugar
- 1 teaspoon salt
- 2 tablespoons olive oil

For the topping:

- 1/4 cup unsalted butter, melted (60g)
- 1/4 cup grated Parmesan cheese (25g)
- 1 tablespoon fresh parsley, chopped
- 1 tablespoon fresh basil, chopped (or 1 teaspoon dried basil)
- 2 garlic cloves, minced
- Salt and pepper to taste

DIRECTIONS

1. Make the dough: In a small bowl, dissolve the yeast in warm water and let it sit for 5-10 minutes until foamy. In a large bowl, combine the flour, sugar, and salt. Add the yeast mixture and olive oil, and mix until a dough forms. Knead the dough on a floured surface for 5-7 minutes, or until smooth and elastic.
2. Let the dough rise: Place the dough in a greased bowl, cover with a damp cloth, and let it rise in a warm place for about 1 hour, or until doubled in size.
3. Shape the knots: Punch down the dough and divide it into 12 equal pieces. Roll each piece into a rope and tie it into a knot. Place the knots on a baking sheet lined with parchment paper.
4. Preheat the oven: Set the oven to 375°F (190°C). Let the knots rise for an additional 10-15 minutes while the oven preheats.
5. Bake the knots: Bake the knots for 12-15 minutes, or until golden brown.
6. Prepare the topping: While the knots are baking, mix the melted butter, grated Parmesan, minced garlic, parsley, and basil in a small bowl.
7. Coat the knots: After removing the knots from the oven, brush them with the Parmesan herb butter mixture. Sprinkle with a bit of extra Parmesan and serve warm.

NOTES

These knots can be stored in an airtight container at room temperature for up to 2 days.

For extra flavor, add a pinch of red pepper flakes to the herb butter mixture.

Cranberry and Walnut Bread

🍴 10-12 slices   🕐 60 minutes

Calories per Serving: 220 kcal
Proteins: 5g
Fats: 10g
Carbs: 30g

INGREDIENTS

For the bread:

- 2 cups all-purpose flour (240g)
- 1/2 cup granulated sugar (100g)
- 1 1/2 teaspoons baking powder
- 1/2 teaspoon baking soda
- 1/2 teaspoon salt
- 1/2 cup unsalted butter, melted (115g)
- 2 large eggs
- 1/2 cup milk (120ml)
- 1/2 teaspoon vanilla extract (2.5ml)
- 1 cup fresh or dried cranberries (120g)
- 1/2 cup chopped walnuts (60g)
- Zest of 1 orange (optional for extra flavor)

DIRECTIONS

1. Preheat the oven: Set the oven to 350°F (175°C). Grease a 9x5-inch loaf pan.
2. Mix dry ingredients: In a large bowl, whisk together the flour, sugar, baking powder, baking soda, and salt.
3. Combine wet ingredients: In a separate bowl, beat the eggs, melted butter, milk, and vanilla extract until smooth.
4. Make the batter: Gradually stir the wet ingredients into the dry ingredients until just combined. Fold in the cranberries, chopped walnuts, and orange zest (if using).
5. Bake: Pour the batter into the prepared loaf pan. Bake for 50-60 minutes, or until a toothpick inserted into the center comes out clean.
6. Cool and serve: Allow the bread to cool in the pan for 10 minutes before transferring to a wire rack to cool completely.

NOTES

This bread can be stored at room temperature for up to 3 days, or frozen for up to 2 months.

Dried cranberries work well if fresh ones aren't available, and you can substitute pecans for walnuts if desired.

- Christmas Appetizer Bakes: Puff Pastry Bites, Savory Scones, and Cheese Straws
  Savory Edible Gifts: Homemade Crackers, Savory Biscotti, and Spiced Nuts

Puff Pastry Bites

24 bites | 15 minutes

Calories per Serving: 80 kcal
Proteins: 2g
Fats: 6g
Carbs: 7g

INGREDIENTS

1 sheet puff pastry, thawed (store-bought or homemade)

1 egg, beaten (for egg wash)

1/2 cup cheese (such as Parmesan, Gruyère, or cheddar)

Optional toppings:
- Sliced cherry tomatoes
- Pesto
- Caramelized onions
- Bacon bits
- Sautéed mushrooms

DIRECTIONS

1. Preheat the oven: Set the oven to 400°F (200°C). Line a baking sheet with parchment paper.
2. Prepare the puff pastry: Roll out the thawed puff pastry sheet on a floured surface. Cut the pastry into 1 1/2-inch squares or rounds using a knife or cookie cutter.
3. Assemble the bites: Place the puff pastry pieces on the prepared baking sheet. Brush each piece with the beaten egg for a golden finish.
4. Add toppings: Sprinkle your choice of cheese and any toppings on each piece of puff pastry.
5. Bake: Bake the puff pastry bites for 12-15 minutes, or until they are puffed and golden brown.
6. Serve: Allow the bites to cool for a few minutes before serving. Enjoy warm or at room temperature.

NOTES

You can customize the bites with a variety of toppings based on the occasion, such as using smoked salmon and cream cheese for a more elegant touch or tomato and mozzarella for a classic flavor.

Puff pastry bites are best enjoyed fresh but can be stored in an airtight container for up to 2 days.

Savory Scones

8 | 15 minutes

Calories per Serving: 250 kcal
Proteins: 8g
Fats: 15g
Carbs: 22g

INGREDIENTS

2 cups all-purpose flour (240g)
1 tablespoon baking powder
1/2 teaspoon salt
1/4 teaspoon ground black pepper
1/4 cup unsalted butter, cold and cubed (60g)
1/2 cup shredded cheddar cheese (60g)
1/4 cup chopped fresh herbs (such as chives, rosemary, or parsley)
1/4 cup cooked and crumbled bacon or ham (optional)
2 large eggs
1/2 cup buttermilk (120ml)

DIRECTIONS

1. Preheat the oven: Set the oven to 400°F (200°C). Line a baking sheet with parchment paper.
2. Mix the dry ingredients: In a large bowl, whisk together the flour, baking powder, salt, and black pepper.
3. Cut in the butter: Add the cold, cubed butter to the flour mixture and rub it in with your fingertips until the mixture resembles coarse crumbs.
4. Add the cheese and herbs: Stir in the shredded cheese, fresh herbs, and bacon or ham (if using).
5. Combine wet ingredients: In a separate bowl, whisk together the eggs and buttermilk. Pour the wet ingredients into the dry mixture and stir until just combined.
6. Shape the scones: Turn the dough out onto a lightly floured surface and pat it into a 1-inch thick circle. Cut into 8 wedges and place them on the prepared baking sheet.
7. Bake: Bake the scones for 15-18 minutes, or until golden brown. Allow to cool slightly before serving.

NOTES

These scones are best served fresh but can be stored in an airtight container for up to 2 days.
Feel free to swap out the cheese and herbs for your favorite flavor combinations, such as cheddar and thyme or goat cheese and dill.

Cheese Straws

24 | 15 minutes

Calories per Serving: 100 kcal
Proteins: 4g
Fats: 6g
Carbs: 8g

INGREDIENTS

2 c1 1/2 cups all-purpose flour (180g)
1/2 teaspoon salt
1/4 teaspoon cayenne pepper
1/2 cup unsalted butter, cold and cubed (115g)
1 1/2 cups sharp cheddar cheese, shredded (180g)
2 tablespoons cold water

DIRECTIONS

1. Preheat the oven: Set the oven to 375°F (190°C). Line a baking sheet with parchment paper.
2. Make the dough: In a bowl, whisk together the flour, salt, and cayenne. Cut in the butter until the mixture resembles coarse crumbs. Stir in the cheese and add water until the dough forms.
3. Shape and bake: Roll the dough into long strips and twist them into straws. Bake for 12-15 minutes, or until crisp and golden.

NOTES

Storage: Cheese straws can be stored in an airtight container for up to a week, making them a great option to prepare ahead of holiday gatherings.

Customization: You can experiment with different types of cheese like sharp cheddar, Parmesan, or even add a hint of cayenne pepper for a spicy kick.

Serving: Serve these cheese straws as an appetizer, snack, or alongside a festive soup or salad for added texture and flavor.

Homemade Crackers

🍴 40 🕐 15 minutes

Calories per Serving: 60 kcal
Proteins: 2g
Fats: 2g
Carbs: 8g

INGREDIENTS

1 1/4 cups all-purpose flour (150g)
1/4 teaspoon salt
2 tablespoons olive oil
1/4 cup water (60ml)
Optional toppings: sesame seeds, sea salt, herbs

DIRECTIONS

1. Preheat the oven: Set the oven to 400°F (200°C). Line a baking sheet with parchment paper.
2. Make the dough: Combine the flour, salt, olive oil, and water in a bowl. Stir until a dough forms.
3. Roll and bake: Roll the dough out thinly, cut into squares, and sprinkle with toppings. Bake for 12-15 minutes, or until golden and crisp.

NOTES

Storage: Store these homemade crackers in an airtight container for up to one week. They retain their crispness and make a great snack for holiday entertaining.

Flavor Variations: Customize the crackers by adding your favorite herbs and spices such as rosemary, thyme, or garlic powder. You can also experiment with different seeds like poppy seeds or flaxseeds for added texture.

Serving: These crackers pair wonderfully with cheese boards, dips, or charcuterie platters, making them ideal for festive gatherings.

Savory Biscotti

24 biscotti | 35 minutes

Calories per Serving: 90 kcal
Proteins: 4g
Fats: 6g
Carbs: 10g

INGREDIENTS

1 1/4 cups all-purpose flour (150g)
1/2 cup grated Parmesan cheese (50g)
1 teaspoon baking powder
1/2 teaspoon salt
1/2 cup unsalted butter, softened (115g)
2 large eggs
1 tablespoon fresh rosemary, chopped
1/4 cup sun-dried tomatoes, chopped (optional)

DIRECTIONS

1. Preheat the oven: Set the oven to 350°F (175°C). Line a baking sheet with parchment paper.
2. Make the dough: In a large bowl, whisk together the flour, Parmesan, baking powder, and salt. Beat the butter and eggs in a separate bowl until creamy, then add to the dry ingredients. Stir in the rosemary and sun-dried tomatoes.
3. Shape and bake: Shape the dough into a log, about 10 inches long. Bake for 25-30 minutes until golden. Remove from the oven, let cool for 10 minutes, then slice into 1/2-inch pieces. Return to the oven for another 8-10 minutes until crisp.

NOTES

Storage: Savory biscotti can be stored in an airtight container for up to two weeks, making them ideal for gifting or preparing ahead of time for holiday gatherings.

Flavor Variations: You can easily customize the biscotti with different flavor combinations such as adding olives, thyme, or even incorporating nuts for added texture.

Serving: These savory biscotti pair well with cheese spreads, dips, or can be served alongside a bowl of warm soup as a crunchy accompaniment.

Spiced Nuts

2 cups | 25 minutes

Calories per Serving: 200 kcal
Proteins: 5g
Fats: 18g
Carbs: 6g

INGREDIENTS

2 cups mixed nuts (almonds, walnuts, pecans)

2 tablespoons olive oil or melted butter

1 tablespoon brown sugar

1 teaspoon ground cumin

1/2 teaspoon smoked paprika

1/4 teaspoon cayenne pepper

1/2 teaspoon salt

DIRECTIONS

1. Preheat the oven: Set the oven to 350°F (175°C). Line a baking sheet with parchment paper.
2. Mix the nuts: In a bowl, toss the nuts with olive oil or melted butter. Add the brown sugar, cumin, smoked paprika, cayenne, and salt, stirring until the nuts are coated.
3. Bake: Spread the nuts in a single layer on the baking sheet. Bake for 20-25 minutes, stirring halfway through, until the nuts are golden and fragrant.

NOTES

Storage: Store spiced nuts in an airtight container for up to two weeks. They make for great edible gifts or a quick holiday snack.

Flavor Variations: Customize the spice blend to your preference by adding ingredients like smoked paprika, rosemary, or even a touch of honey for sweetness.

Serving Suggestions: Serve these spiced nuts at holiday gatherings alongside cheese boards or as part of a snack platter.

Chapter 4: Specialty Diets – Gluten-Free, Vegan & Dairy-Free Bakes

The holidays are a time to gather and share joy with everyone, and that includes offering delicious treats for all dietary needs. In this chapter, we focus on creating gluten-free, vegan, and dairy-free bakes that ensure no one misses out on the festive flavors. From rich, indulgent cakes to wholesome cookies, these recipes prove that dietary restrictions don't mean compromising on taste or presentation. Whether you're baking for yourself or loved ones with specific dietary requirements, these recipes will help you create inclusive, delightful treats that everyone at the table can enjoy.

Almond Flour Snowballs

🍴 24 cookies 🕐 15 minutes

Calories per Serving: 100 kcal
Proteins: 2g
Fats: 8g
Carbs: 5g

INGREDIENTS

2 cups almond flour (200g)

1/4 cup powdered sugar (30g) (plus extra for rolling)

1/4 teaspoon salt

1/2 cup unsalted butter, softened (115g)

1 teaspoon vanilla extract (5ml)

1/2 cup chopped almonds or walnuts (optional)

DIRECTIONS

1. Preheat the oven: Set the oven to 350°F (175°C) and line a baking sheet with parchment paper.
2. Make the dough: In a large bowl, cream together the softened butter, powdered sugar, and vanilla extract until smooth. Stir in the almond flour and salt until well combined. Fold in the chopped nuts (if using).
3. Shape the cookies: Roll the dough into 1-inch balls and place them on the prepared baking sheet about 1 inch apart.
4. Bake: Bake for 12-15 minutes, or until the edges are lightly golden. Let the cookies cool for 5 minutes on the baking sheet before rolling them in powdered sugar while still warm.
5. Coat again: Once completely cooled, roll the cookies in powdered sugar a second time for an extra snowy finish.

NOTES

These cookies can be stored in an airtight container at room temperature for up to a week.

For an extra festive flavor, add 1/4 teaspoon of cinnamon or nutmeg to the dough.

Gluten-Free Ginger Snaps

🍴 24 cookies   🕒 15 minutes

Calories per Serving: 80 kcal
Proteins: 1g
Fats: 3g
Carbs: 12g

INGREDIENTS

2 1/4 cups almond flour (150g)
1/2 cup coconut flour (60g)
1/2 teaspoon baking soda
1/4 teaspoon salt
1 tablespoon ground ginger
1 teaspoon ground cinnamon
1/4 teaspoon ground cloves
1/4 cup unsalted butter, softened (60g)
1/4 cup molasses (60ml)
1/4 cup maple syrup (60ml)
1 large egg
1 teaspoon vanilla extract (5ml)

DIRECTIONS

1. Preheat the oven: Set the oven to 350°F (175°C) and line a baking sheet with parchment paper.
2. Mix dry ingredients: In a bowl, whisk together the almond flour, coconut flour, baking soda, salt, ginger, cinnamon, and cloves.
3. Mix wet ingredients: In another bowl, beat the softened butter with molasses, maple syrup, and vanilla extract until smooth. Add the egg and beat until fully incorporated.
4. Combine wet and dry ingredients: Gradually mix the dry ingredients into the wet mixture until a dough forms.
5. Shape the cookies: Roll the dough into 1-inch balls and place them on the prepared baking sheet, flattening each one slightly with your hand.
6. Bake: Bake for 10-12 minutes, or until the edges are lightly golden. Let the cookies cool on the baking sheet for a few minutes before transferring to a wire rack to cool completely.

NOTES

Store the cookies in an airtight container at room temperature for up to a week.
You can make the cookies crisper by baking them an additional minute or two, or leave them a bit softer by slightly underbaking.

Egg-Free Fruitcake

12-16 slices | 120 minutes

Calories per Serving: 250 kcal
Proteins: 3g
Fats: 7g
Carbs: 45g

INGREDIENTS

1 1/2 cups all-purpose flour (180g)
1 teaspoon baking powder
1/2 teaspoon baking soda
1 teaspoon ground cinnamon
1/2 teaspoon ground nutmeg
1/2 teaspoon ground cloves
1/2 cup unsweetened applesauce (120ml)
1/2 cup vegetable oil (120ml)
1/2 cup brown sugar (100g)
1/4 cup orange juice (60ml)
1 cup mixed dried fruits (such as raisins, currants, and chopped apricots) (150g)
1/2 cup chopped nuts (optional) (60g)
1 teaspoon vanilla extract (5ml)

DIRECTIONS

1. Preheat the oven: Set the oven to 325°F (160°C) and grease a loaf pan or a small cake pan.
2. Combine dry ingredients: In a large bowl, whisk together the flour, baking powder, baking soda, cinnamon, nutmeg, and cloves.
3. Mix wet ingredients: In a separate bowl, combine the applesauce, vegetable oil, brown sugar, and orange juice. Stir in the vanilla extract.
4. Combine wet and dry ingredients: Gradually fold the wet ingredients into the dry ingredients until just combined. Stir in the dried fruits and chopped nuts.
5. Bake: Pour the batter into the prepared pan and bake for 1 1/2 to 2 hours, or until a toothpick inserted into the center comes out clean. Let the fruitcake cool in the pan for 10 minutes before transferring to a wire rack to cool completely.

NOTES

This egg-free fruitcake can be stored in an airtight container at room temperature for up to 1 week, or in the fridge for longer freshness.

For an extra flavor boost, soak the dried fruits in orange juice or brandy overnight before mixing into the batter.

Vegan Chocolate Yule Log

10-12 slices   18 minutes

Calories per Serving: 250 kcal
Proteins: 5g
Fats: 12g
Carbs: 32g

INGREDIENTS

For the sponge cake:
- 1 cup all-purpose flour (120g)
- 1/4 cup cocoa powder (25g)
- 1 teaspoon baking powder
- 1/4 teaspoon salt
- 1/2 cup granulated sugar (100g)
- 1/2 cup plant-based milk (such as almond or soy) (120ml)
- 1/4 cup vegetable oil (60ml)
- 1 teaspoon vanilla extract (5ml)
- 1 tablespoon apple cider vinegar or lemon juice (to create a vegan "buttermilk")

For the filling:
- 1 cup coconut cream (240ml)
- 1/4 cup powdered sugar (30g)
- 1 teaspoon vanilla extract (5ml)

For the chocolate ganache:
- 1 cup vegan dark chocolate, chopped (175g)
- 1/2 cup coconut milk (120ml)

NOTES

This cake can be made a day ahead and stored in the fridge until ready to serve. Garnish with fresh berries or edible flowers for an extra festive touch.

DIRECTIONS

1. Preheat the oven: Set the oven to 350°F (175°C) and line a 10x15-inch jelly roll pan with parchment paper.
2. Make the vegan buttermilk: In a small bowl, mix the plant-based milk and apple cider vinegar (or lemon juice) and let it sit for 5 minutes to curdle.
3. Mix the dry ingredients: In a large bowl, whisk together the flour, cocoa powder, baking powder, salt, and sugar.
4. Combine wet and dry ingredients: Add the vegan buttermilk, vegetable oil, and vanilla extract to the dry ingredients and mix until just combined. Pour the batter into the prepared pan and spread it evenly.
5. Bake: Bake the cake for 15-18 minutes, or until a toothpick inserted into the center comes out clean. Let the cake cool slightly before rolling it up in a clean kitchen towel dusted with powdered sugar. Let it cool completely.
6. Prepare the filling: While the cake cools, whip the coconut cream with powdered sugar and vanilla extract until fluffy. Unroll the cake and spread the coconut cream over the surface. Roll the cake back up without the towel.
7. Make the chocolate ganache: Heat the coconut milk until simmering, then pour it over the chopped vegan dark chocolate. Let it sit for 1-2 minutes, then stir until smooth.
8. Frost the Yule Log: Spread the chocolate ganache over the rolled cake, creating a bark-like texture using a fork. Chill in the fridge for at least 1 hour before serving.

Dairy-Free Cheesecake

12 slices | 60 minutes

Calories per Serving: 300 kcal
Proteins: 6g
Fats: 18g
Carbs: 32g

INGREDIENTS

For the crust:
- 1 1/2 cups graham cracker crumbs (150g) (use dairy-free crackers)
- 1/4 cup coconut oil or dairy-free butter, melted (60ml)
- 2 tablespoons sugar

For the filling:
- 16 oz dairy-free cream cheese (such as Tofutti or Kite Hill)
- 1 cup full-fat coconut milk (240ml)
- 3/4 cup granulated sugar (150g)
- 1 tablespoon cornstarch
- 1 teaspoon vanilla extract (5ml)
- Zest of 1 lemon (optional)

DIRECTIONS

1. Prepare the crust: Preheat the oven to 325°F (160°C). In a bowl, mix graham cracker crumbs, melted coconut oil, and sugar. Press the mixture into the bottom of a 9-inch springform pan. Bake for 8-10 minutes, then let it cool.
2. Make the filling: In a large bowl, beat the dairy-free cream cheese, coconut milk, sugar, cornstarch, and vanilla extract until smooth. Pour the filling over the crust.
3. Bake: Bake for 50-60 minutes, or until the edges are set and the center is slightly jiggly. Turn off the oven and leave the cheesecake inside for 1 hour. Let it cool completely, then refrigerate for at least 4 hours or overnight before serving.

Vegan Pumpkin Pie

🍴 8 slices   🕐 55 minutes

Calories per Serving: 240 kcal
Proteins: 4g
Fats: 12g
Carbs: 32g

INGREDIENTS

·For the crust:
- 1 1/2 cups all-purpose flour (180g)
- 1/2 cup coconut oil, solid (115g)
- 2-4 tablespoons cold water

·For the filling:
- 1 can pumpkin purée (15 oz/425g)
- 1 cup coconut milk (240ml)
- 3/4 cup maple syrup (180ml)
- 1 tablespoon cornstarch
- 1 teaspoon ground cinnamon
- 1/2 teaspoon ground ginger
- 1/4 teaspoon ground cloves
- 1/2 teaspoon vanilla extract

DIRECTIONS

1. Prepare the crust: Preheat the oven to 350°F (175°C). In a bowl, combine the flour and solid coconut oil, rubbing it in until crumbly. Add cold water 1 tablespoon at a time until the dough comes together. Roll it out and press into a pie dish. Blind bake for 10 minutes.
2. Make the filling: In a large bowl, whisk together pumpkin purée, coconut milk, maple syrup, cornstarch, spices, and vanilla extract.
3. Assemble and bake: Pour the pumpkin mixture into the pre-baked crust. Bake for 50-55 minutes, or until the center is set. Allow it to cool before serving.

NOTES

Storage: Vegan pumpkin pie can be stored in the refrigerator for up to 4-5 days. Be sure to cover it tightly to maintain freshness.
Serving Suggestions: Serve with a dollop of dairy-free whipped cream or a sprinkle of cinnamon for an extra festive touch.
Customization: For added flavor, try adding a pinch of nutmeg or ginger to the filling. You can also garnish with crushed pecans or a drizzle of maple syrup.

Nut-Free Biscotti

24 biscotti • 30 minutes

Calories per Serving: 80 kcal
Proteins: 2g
Fats: 2g
Carbs: 15g

INGREDIENTS

2 cups all-purpose flour (240g)
1 teaspoon baking powder
1/4 teaspoon salt
3/4 cup granulated sugar (150g)
1/2 cup unsalted butter, softened (115g)
2 large eggs
1 teaspoon vanilla extract
Zest of 1 lemon or orange (optional)
1/2 cup dried fruit (such as cranberries, cherries, or raisins)

DIRECTIONS

1. Preheat the oven: Set the oven to 350°F (175°C) and line a baking sheet with parchment paper.
2. Make the dough: In a bowl, whisk together the flour, baking powder, and salt. In another bowl, beat the butter and sugar until fluffy. Add eggs, vanilla extract, and citrus zest (if using). Stir in the dry ingredients and dried fruit until a dough forms.
3. Shape and bake: Divide the dough in half and shape into two logs. Bake for 25-30 minutes, until golden. Let cool, then slice into biscotti shapes and bake for an additional 8-10 minutes to crisp them up.

NOTES

Storage: These biscotti can be stored in an airtight container for up to two weeks, making them perfect for gifting or preparing ahead of time.
Flavor Variations: Instead of nuts, try adding dried fruits like cranberries, cherries, or even chocolate chips for a delicious twist.
Serving Suggestions: Nut-free biscotti pair wonderfully with coffee or tea, and they make an excellent addition to holiday gift baskets.

Vegan Chocolate Bark

🍴 16 pieces 🕐 120 minutes

Calories per
Serving: 150 kcal
Proteins: 2g
Fats: 9g
Carbs: 15g

INGREDIENTS

2 cups vegan dark chocolate (chopped or chips) (300g)

1/4 cup dried fruit (such as cranberries or raisins)

1/4 cup pumpkin seeds or sunflower seeds (to keep it nut-free)

1 tablespoon coconut flakes (optional)

1/4 teaspoon sea salt (optional)

DIRECTIONS

1. Melt the chocolate: In a microwave or using a double boiler, melt the vegan dark chocolate until smooth.
2. Spread the chocolate: Pour the melted chocolate onto a parchment-lined baking sheet and spread it into an even layer.
3. Add toppings: Sprinkle the dried fruit, seeds, coconut flakes, and sea salt evenly over the chocolate.
4. Chill and break: Refrigerate for 1-2 hours or until the chocolate is set. Once firm, break the bark into pieces.

NOTES

Storage: These biscotti can be stored in an airtight container for up to two weeks, making them perfect for gifting or preparing ahead of time.

Flavor Variations: Instead of nuts, try adding dried fruits like cranberries, cherries, or even chocolate chips for a delicious twist.

Serving Suggestions: Nut-free biscotti pair wonderfully with coffee or tea, and they make an excellent addition to holiday gift baskets.

Substitution Guide: How to Adapt Traditional Recipes for Specialty Diets

1. Egg Substitutes (for Vegan or Egg-Free Recipes):

- Flaxseed or Chia Seed: Mix 1 tablespoon of ground flaxseed or chia seeds with 3 tablespoons of water. Let it sit for 5 minutes to create a gel-like consistency. This works well in cookies, muffins, and cakes.
- Unsweetened Applesauce: Replace 1 egg with 1/4 cup of applesauce in baked goods like cakes and brownies.
- Mashed Banana: Use 1/4 cup of mashed banana per egg for moisture and binding, especially in dense baked goods like pancakes or banana bread.
- Aquafaba: Use 3 tablespoons of the liquid from canned chickpeas as a substitute for 1 egg in recipes requiring egg whites like meringues or macarons.

2. Dairy Substitutes (for Dairy-Free or Vegan Recipes):

- Milk: Replace cow's milk with plant-based alternatives such as almond, soy, oat, or coconut milk. Use in a 1:1 ratio in any recipe.
- Butter: Use coconut oil, vegan butter, or olive oil as a substitute for butter in baked goods. Coconut oil works well in cookies and cakes, while vegan butter is great for frosting and pastries.
- Cheese: Replace dairy cheese with nut-based or soy-based vegan cheeses in savory recipes like lasagna or quiche.
- Cream: Swap heavy cream with full-fat coconut milk in soups, sauces, or desserts. Coconut cream also works well in whipped cream recipes.

3. Gluten Substitutes (for Gluten-Free Recipes):

- Flour: Use gluten-free flour blends, almond flour, or oat flour in place of regular wheat flour. Some common pre-made gluten-free blends contain rice flour, tapioca starch, and potato starch for a 1:1 substitution.
- Bread Crumbs: Replace traditional bread crumbs with gluten-free panko, crushed gluten-free crackers, or almond meal in recipes like meatloaf or breaded dishes.

Pasta: Swap wheat-based pasta for gluten-free alternatives made from rice, corn, or quinoa. Most grocery stores carry a variety of gluten-free pasta options that cook similarly to traditional pasta.

4. Sugar Substitutes (for Low-Sugar or Diabetic-Friendly Recipes):
   - Stevia or Monk Fruit: Use stevia or monk fruit as natural sweeteners in baked goods, sauces, or drinks. Both are much sweeter than sugar, so check conversion ratios (usually 1/2 teaspoon of stevia for 1 cup of sugar).
   - Maple Syrup or Honey: For a natural alternative, use honey or maple syrup in place of sugar, adjusting liquids in the recipe accordingly.
   - Coconut Sugar: A lower-glycemic alternative that works in a 1:1 ratio with white or brown sugar.

5. Fat Substitutes (for Low-Fat or Heart-Healthy Recipes):
   - Avocado: Replace butter or oil with mashed avocado in baked goods like brownies or muffins. Use in a 1:1 ratio for a creamy, healthy fat alternative.
   - Greek Yogurt: Use Greek yogurt in place of butter or oil in cakes or muffins for added moisture without extra fat.
   - Applesauce: Swap oil or butter for unsweetened applesauce in baked goods. This works especially well in cakes, muffins, and quick breads.

6. Meat Substitutes (for Vegan or Vegetarian Recipes):
   - Tofu or Tempeh: Use tofu or tempeh in place of meat in stir-fries, curries, and sandwiches. These plant-based proteins absorb marinades and sauces well and are packed with protein.
   - Lentils or Chickpeas: Replace ground meat in chili, tacos, or burgers with lentils or chickpeas. They provide a similar texture and are high in protein and fiber.
   - Seitan: Use seitan (wheat gluten) in place of beef or chicken in hearty dishes like stews or roasts. It has a chewy texture and works well in savory recipes

Chapter 5: Festive Drinks

No holiday gathering is complete without a selection of warm, comforting drinks to accompany the festive treats. In this chapter, you'll discover a collection of drinks that bring the holiday spirit to life—ranging from the cozy richness of mulled wine to the indulgent warmth of peppermint hot chocolate. These festive drinks not only warm the soul but pair beautifully with the variety of holiday bakes featured in earlier chapters. Whether you're hosting a party or enjoying a quiet evening by the fire, these drinks will add an extra layer of joy and celebration to your holiday season.

Classic Mulled Wine

INGREDIENTS

1 bottle of red wine
1 orange (sliced)
3 cinnamon sticks
4 cloves
2-star anise
1/4 cup sugar (optional)
1/4 cup brandy (optional)

DIRECTIONS

1. Combine the wine, orange slices, cinnamon sticks, cloves, star anise, and sugar in a large pot.
2. Simmer gently over low heat for 20-30 minutes, ensuring the wine doesn't boil.
3. Stir in the brandy (optional) and serve warm.

Holiday Punch (Non-Alcoholic):

INGREDIENTS

4 cups cranberry juice
2 cups orange juice
1 cup pineapple juice
2 cups sparkling water
Orange slices, cranberries, and pomegranate seeds for garnish

DIRECTIONS

1. In a large punch bowl, combine the juices.
2. Add the sparkling water just before serving to keep it fizzy.
3. Garnish with orange slices, cranberries, and pomegranate seeds.

Cranberry Rum Punch

INGREDIENTS

3 cups cranberry juice
1 cup orange juice
1 cup pineapple juice
1/2 cup light rum
1/2 cup dark rum
1/4 cup lime juice
1/4 cup simple syrup
Fresh cranberries and orange slices for garnish

DIRECTIONS

1. Combine cranberry juice, orange juice, pineapple juice, lime juice, and simple syrup in a large punch bowl.
2. Add light and dark rum, stirring well.
3. Chill for at least 2 hours before serving.
4. Garnish with fresh cranberries and orange slices. Serve over ice.

Spiked Holiday Sangria Punch

INGREDIENTS

3 1 bottle red wine
1 cup brandy
2 cups orange juice
1/4 cup triple sec
1/4 cup simple syrup
1 cup club soda
Fresh orange slices, pomegranate seeds, and cinnamon sticks for garnish

DIRECTIONS

1. In a large pitcher, combine the red wine, brandy, orange juice, triple sec, and simple syrup.
2. Chill for 1-2 hours.
3. Just before serving, add the club soda for fizz.
4. Garnish with orange slices, pomegranate seeds, and cinnamon sticks.

Champagne Holiday Punch

INGREDIENTS

1 bottle champagne or prosecco
2 cups cranberry juice
1/4 cup Grand Marnier or Cointreau
1/4 cup vodka
1/4 cup simple syrup
Fresh mint and cranberries for garnish

DIRECTIONS

1. In a punch bowl, combine cranberry juice, Grand Marnier, vodka, and simple syrup.
2. Gently pour in the champagne just before serving.
3. Garnish with fresh mint and cranberries.

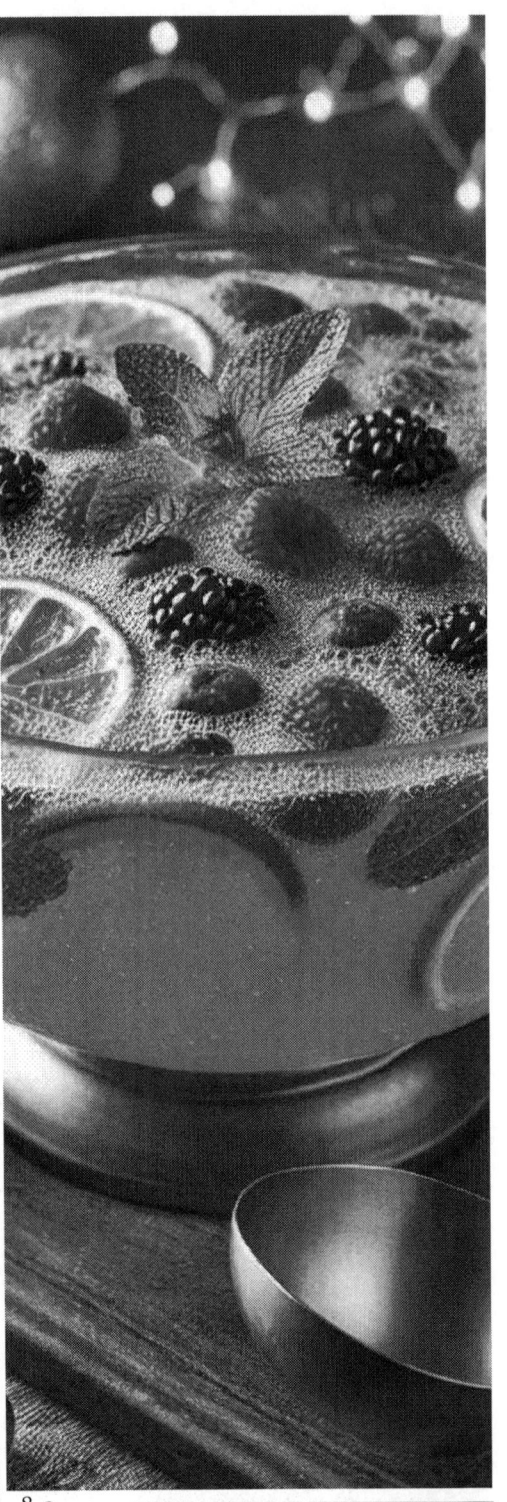

Peppermint Hot Cocoa

INGREDIENTS

4 cups almond milk (or milk of choice)
1/2 cup cocoa powder
1/4 cup sugar
1/4 teaspoon peppermint extract
Whipped cream and crushed candy canes for topping

DIRECTIONS

1. In a saucepan, whisk together the milk, cocoa powder, and sugar over medium heat until smooth.
2. Stir in the peppermint extract.
3. Serve with whipped cream and crushed candy canes.

Spiced Mexican Hot Chocolate

INGREDIENTS

4 cups almond milk (or milk of choice)
1/2 cup unsweetened cocoa powder
1/4 cup sugar (adjust to taste)
1/2 teaspoon ground cinnamon
1/4 teaspoon ground nutmeg
1/8 teaspoon cayenne pepper (optional, for a kick)
1 teaspoon vanilla extract
3 oz dark chocolate, chopped (use dairy-free chocolate for a vegan version)
Whipped cream, cinnamon sticks, or chocolate shavings for garnish

DIRECTIONS

1. In a medium saucepan, heat the almond milk over medium heat until warm (do not boil).
2. Whisk in the cocoa powder, sugar, cinnamon, nutmeg, and cayenne pepper. Stir until well combined and smooth.
3. Add the chopped dark chocolate and vanilla extract, stirring constantly until the chocolate has melted and the mixture is smooth and creamy.
4. Remove from heat and pour into mugs.
5. Garnish with whipped cream, cinnamon sticks, or chocolate shavings for an extra festive touch.

Traditional Eggnog

INGREDIENTS

- 4 egg yolks
- 1/2 cup sugar
- 2 cups whole milk
- 1 cup heavy cream
- 1/2 teaspoon nutmeg
- 1/2 teaspoon vanilla extract
- 1/4 cup rum or bourbon (optional)

DIRECTIONS

1. Whisk egg yolks and sugar until light and fluffy.
2. Heat the milk and cream in a saucepan, then slowly add it to the egg mixture while whisking.
3. Return the mixture to the pan, add nutmeg, and cook until slightly thickened.
4. Stir in vanilla and alcohol (optional). Chill before serving.

Mulled Apple Cider:

INGREDIENTS

4 cups apple cider
1 orange (sliced)
2 cinnamon sticks
4 cloves
1-star anise
1 tablespoon honey (optional)

DIRECTIONS

1. Combine apple cider, orange slices, cinnamon sticks, cloves, and star anise in a pot.
2. Simmer over low heat for 20-30 minutes.
3. Sweeten with honey if desired.

Chapter 6: Creative Presentation Ideas for Edible Gifts

One of the joys of holiday baking is sharing your creations with others, and presentation plays a key role in turning homemade treats into thoughtful gifts. In this chapter, you'll explore creative ways to wrap, decorate, and present your baked goods, making them as beautiful as they are delicious. Whether you're crafting personalized gift tags, arranging festive cookie baskets, or preparing elegant packaging for edible gifts, these ideas will help you add that special touch to your holiday presents. With a little extra attention to detail, your treats will not only taste amazing but also become a cherished part of the holiday experience.

Festive Packaging Tips: How to Wrap and Present Your Baked Goods

1. Decorative Tins and Boxes:

Use festive tins, cookie boxes, or small decorative crates to package your treats.

Line the tins with parchment paper or colorful tissue paper to cushion the baked goods and add a pop of color.

Look for holiday-themed boxes with clear lids that allow the recipient to see the treats inside.

2. Glass Jars for Layered Ingredients:

For cookie or cake mixes, use mason jars to layer dry ingredients like flour, sugar, and chocolate chips. Add a ribbon and attach a tag with the baking instructions.

You can also use jars for pre-made treats like truffles, mini cookies, or spiced nuts.

3. Cellophane Bags and Ribbons:

Stack cookies or bars in clear cellophane bags tied with festive ribbons or twine.

Add decorative elements like sprigs of pine, cinnamon sticks, or candy canes for an extra holiday touch.

4. Parchment Paper Wraps:

Use parchment paper or wax paper to wrap individual treats or baked goods like breads and cakes.

Secure the wrap with baker's twine, and add a wax seal or a personalized label for a rustic, elegant look.

Personalized Gift Tags and Labels: Free Printables and Design Tips

1. Create Custom Labels:

Use online design tools like Canva or Adobe Spark to create personalized gift tags and labels. Add festive colors, holiday icons, and space for handwritten messages.

Include the name of the treat, ingredients (in case of dietary restrictions), and a personal message or holiday greeting.

2. Printable Holiday Tags:

Offer a variety of downloadable and printable holiday gift tags in different themes (rustic, modern, traditional). You can find free printables on sites like Pinterest, or create your own set to match the theme of your book. Laminate or print on heavy card stock for durability.

3. Handwritten Labels:

If you prefer a more personal touch, use kraft paper labels or gift tags for handwritten messages.

Include the recipe name, serving suggestions, or a holiday greeting. Embellish with stamps, stickers, or metallic pens.

Gift Basket Ideas: How to Create a Festive Gift Basket with Your Bakes

1. Curate a Themed Basket:

Choose a theme for your gift basket (e.g., "Holiday Baking Essentials," "Cookie Lover's Basket," "Winter Warmers") and select complementary baked goods.

Include a mix of your baked treats (like biscotti, cookies, and fruitcake) along with extras like hot cocoa mix, a mini whisk, or festive tea towels.

2. Layering the Basket:

Line the bottom of the basket with shredded paper or crinkle fill to create a base.

Arrange the baked goods in different containers (small tins, jars, or wrapped bundles) and position them at various heights to create visual interest.

3. Add Decorative Touches:

Use ribbons, bows, and ornaments to add festive flair. Tie a holiday card or recipe card to the basket with a ribbon.

Include seasonal touches like cinnamon sticks, small pinecones, or a sprig of fresh rosemary or holly for fragrance and decoration.

Chapter 7: Leftovers Reimagined

The holiday season often leaves us with an abundance of delicious leftovers, and rather than letting them go to waste, this chapter is dedicated to reimagining those leftovers into exciting new dishes. From savory hand pies filled with turkey and cranberry sauce to sweet, indulgent treats like fruitcake bread pudding, you'll discover creative ways to transform your holiday extras into fresh meals that everyone will love. These recipes breathe new life into familiar ingredients, making post-holiday cooking a breeze and ensuring that nothing goes to waste. Get ready to turn your leftovers into something extraordinary!

Christmas Pudding Truffles

Turn leftover Christmas Pudding into rich, indulgent truffles.

INGREDIENTS

Leftover Christmas pudding (about 2 cups)
1/4 cup dark chocolate, melted
1/4 cup cream (or dairy-free alternative)
1 tablespoon brandy or rum (optional)
Cocoa powder or crushed nuts for coating

DIRECTIONS

1. Crumble the pudding: In a large bowl, crumble the leftover Christmas pudding into fine pieces.
2. Mix in chocolate and cream: Add the melted dark chocolate and cream to the crumbled pudding. Stir until the mixture is well-combined and smooth. Add a splash of brandy or rum if desired.
3. Shape and coat: Roll the mixture into small truffle-sized balls and coat them in cocoa powder or crushed nuts.
4. Chill: Place the truffles in the fridge to set for at least 30 minutes before serving.

Pairing: These truffles pair beautifully with a cup of coffee or hot chocolate.

Turkey and Cranberry Hand Pies

Savory hand pies are a great way to repurpose turkey and cranberry sauce into a handheld treat.

INGREDIENTS

Leftover cooked turkey (about 2 cups, shredded)
1/2 cup cranberry sauce
1/2 cup mashed potatoes (optional)
1 sheet puff pastry (or pie dough)
1 egg (for egg wash)

DIRECTIONS

1. Preheat oven: Set the oven to 375°F (190°C).
2. Prepare the filling: In a bowl, mix the shredded turkey with cranberry sauce and mashed potatoes if using.
3. Assemble the pies: Roll out the puff pastry and cut it into squares or circles. Place a spoonful of the turkey mixture in the center of each piece, then fold over and seal the edges.
4. Brush with egg wash: Brush the tops of the hand pies with a beaten egg for a golden finish.
5. Bake: Bake for 20-25 minutes until golden and flaky.

Pairing: These hand pies are perfect served with a side of gravy or extra cranberry sauce.

Fruitcake Bread Pudding

A Cozy Dessert to Use Up Leftovers

INGREDIENTS

2 cups leftover fruitcake, cubed
2 cups milk (or a dairy-free alternative)
2 eggs
1/4 cup sugar
1 teaspoon vanilla extract
1/2 teaspoon cinnamon

DIRECTIONS

1. Preheat oven: Set the oven to 350°F (175°C) and grease a baking dish.
2. Prepare the custard: In a bowl, whisk together the milk, eggs, sugar, vanilla, and cinnamon.
3. Assemble the pudding: Place the cubed fruitcake in the baking dish and pour the custard mixture over it, ensuring the cake is soaked.
4. Bake: Bake for 30-35 minutes or until the custard is set and the top is golden brown.

Pairing: Serve warm with a drizzle of caramel sauce or a dollop of whipped cream.

Leftover Cookies Crumble

Transform leftover cookies into a versatile crumb crust or topping for other desserts, such as cheesecakes, pies, or ice cream.

INGREDIENTS

Leftover cookies (about 2 cups, crumbled)
1/4 cup melted butter
2 tablespoons sugar (optional)

DIRECTIONS

1. Crumble the cookies: Place the leftover cookies in a food processor and pulse until they are finely crumbled.
2. Combine: Mix the cookie crumbs with melted butter and sugar if desired.
3. Use as a crust: Press the mixture into a pie dish or cheesecake pan to form a crust, then bake for 10-12 minutes until golden.
4. Use as a topping: Alternatively, use the cookie crumble as a topping for ice cream or yogurt parfaits.

Pairing: This crumb crust is ideal for cheesecakes, tarts, or simply as a snack topping.

Conclusion: A Sweet and Savory Holiday Farewell

As we come to the close of this baking journey, I hope this collection of festive recipes has inspired you to celebrate the holiday season with warmth, flavor, and creativity. From delicate cookies and showstopping cakes to savory bakes and inventive ways to use leftovers, each recipe is designed to bring joy to your table and smiles to those you love.

Whether you're creating edible gifts for friends and family, experimenting with new flavors, or turning leftovers into something special, these recipes offer endless possibilities for festive baking. The holiday season is a time for togetherness, and nothing brings people together quite like the comforting aroma of fresh-baked treats and the shared joy of giving homemade gifts.

As you continue baking through the holidays, may these recipes become a cherished part of your traditions, adding magic to your celebrations for years to come. Wishing you a warm, sweet, and savory holiday season filled with love and delicious moments!

Printed in Great Britain
by Amazon